P9-DMK-115

CAREER IDEAS
for kids who like
MUSIC AND DANCE

DIANE LINDSEY REEVES
WITH
GAYLE BRYAN

Illustrations by
NANCY BOND

Facts On File, Inc.

CAREER IDEAS FOR KIDS WHO LIKE MUSIC AND DANCE

Facts On File, Inc.
132 West 31st Street
New York NY 10001

Library of Congress Cataloging-in-Publication Data

Reeves, Diane Lindsey, 1959–
    Career ideas for kids who like music and dance / Diane Lindsey Reeves ; with Gayle Bryan ; illustrations by Nancy Bond.
        p.   cm. — (Career ideas for kids who like)
    Includes bibliographical references and index.
    ISBN 0-8160-4323-X
        1. Music—Vocational guidance—Juvenile literature. 2. Dance—Vocational guidance—Juvenile literature. [1. Music—Vocational guidance. 2. Dance—Vocational guidance. 3. Vocational guidance.]
    I. Bond, Nancy ill. II. Title.

ML3795.2.R43 2001   00-052793

Facts On File books are available at special discounts when purchased in bulk quantities for businesses, associations, institutions or sales promotions. Please call our Special Sales Department in New York at 212/967-8800 or 800/322-8755.

You can find Facts On File on the World Wide Web at http://www.factsonfile.com

Text and cover design by Smart Graphics
Illustrations by Nancy Bond

This book is printed on acid-free paper.

Printed in the United States of America

MP FOF 10 9 8 7 6 5 4 3 2

To Connie Hansen and
Beverly Atkinson,
proof that old friends
are the best friends.
—DLR

ACKNOWLEDGMENTS

A million thanks to those who took the time to invest in young lives by sharing their stories about work and providing photos for this book:

Preston Bailey
Jason Blume
LeVon Campbell
Laura Cochran
Eddie Coker
Elizabeth Droessler
Gigi Greco
Jerri Goldstein
Ronda Grim
Derek Jones
Paul T. Kwami
John David Peters
Lydia Smith
Michael Tarsia
Kirstie Tice

Also, special thanks to the design team of Smart Graphics, Nancy Bond, and Cathy Rincon for bringing the Career Ideas for Kids series to life with their creative talent.

Finally, much appreciation and admiration is due to all the behind-the-scenes people at Facts On File who have done so much to make this series all that it is. This is especially true for my editor, Nicole Bowen, who has championed this project from day one.

CONTENTS

MAKE A CHOICE!

You're young. Most of your life is still ahead of you. How are you supposed to know what you want to be when you grow up?

You're right: 10, 11, 12, 13 is a bit young to know exactly what and where and how you're going to do whatever it is you're going to do as an adult. But, it's the perfect time to start making some important discoveries about who you are, what you like to do, and what you do best. It's the ideal time to start thinking about what you *want* to do.

Make a choice! If you get a head start now, you may avoid setbacks and mistakes later on.

When it comes to picking a career, you've basically got two choices.

CHOICE A

Wait until you're in college to start figuring out what you want to do. Even then you still may not decide what's up your alley, so you graduate and jump from job to job still searching for something you really like.

Hey, it could work. It might be fun. Lots of (probably most) people do it this way.

The problem is that if you pick Choice A, you may end up settling for second best. You may miss out on a meaningful education, satisfying work, and the rewards of a focused and well-planned career.

You have another choice to consider.

CHOICE B

Start now figuring out your options and thinking about the things that are most important in your life's work: Serving others? Staying true to your values? Making lots of money? Enjoying your work? Your young years are the perfect time to mess around with different career ideas without messing up your life.

Reading this book is a great idea for kids who choose B. It's a first step toward choosing a career that matches your skills, interests, and lifetime goals. It will help you make a plan for tailoring your junior and high school years to fit your career dreams. To borrow a jingle from the U.S. Army—using this book is a way to discover how to "be all that you can be."

Ready for the challenge of Choice B? If so, read the next section to find out how this book can help start you on your way.

HOW TO USE THIS BOOK

This isn't a book about interesting careers that other people have. It's a book about interesting careers that you can have.

Of course, it won't do you a bit of good to just read this book. To get the whole shebang, you're going to have to jump in with both feet, roll up your sleeves, put on your thinking cap—whatever it takes—to help you do these three things:

☀ **Discover** what you do best and enjoy the most. (This is the secret ingredient for finding work that's perfect for you.)

- ☼ **Explore** ways to match your interests and abilities with career ideas.
- ☼ **Experiment** with lots of different ideas until you find the ideal career. (It's like trying on all kinds of hats to see which ones fit!)

Use this book as a road map to some exciting career destinations. Here's what to expect in the chapters that follow.

GET IN GEAR!

First stop: self-discovery. These activities will help you uncover important clues about the special traits and abilities that make you *you*. When you are finished you will have developed a personal Skill Set that will help guide you to career ideas in the next chapter.

TAKE A TRIP!

Next stop: exploration. Cruise down the career idea highway and find out about a variety of career ideas that are especially appropriate for people who like music and dance. Use the Skill Set chart at the beginning of each entry to match your own interests with those required for success on the job.

CONDUCT A MUSICAL DETOUR!

Here's your chance to explore up-and-coming opportunities in the entertainment world with some ideas that put a whole new spin on the notion of "singing for your supper."

DON'T STOP NOW!

Third stop: experimentation. The library, the telephone, a computer, and a mentor—four keys to a successful career-

planning adventure. Use them well, and before long you'll be on the trail of some hot career ideas.

WHAT'S NEXT?

Make a plan! Chart your course (or at least the next stop) with these career-planning road maps. Whether you're moving full steam ahead with a great idea or get slowed down at a yellow light of indecision, these road maps will keep you moving forward toward a great future.

Use a pencil—you're bound to make a detour or two along the way. But, hey, you've got to start somewhere.

HOORAY! YOU DID IT!

Some final rules of the road before sending you off to new adventures.

SOME FUTURE DESTINATIONS

This section lists a few career-planning tools you'll want to know about.

You've got a lot of ground to cover in this phase of your career-planning journey. Start your engines and get ready for an exciting adventure!

Career planning is a lifelong journey. There's usually more than one way to get where you're going, and there are often some interesting detours along the way. But, you have to start somewhere. So, rev up and find out all you can about you—one-of-a-kind, specially designed you. That's the first stop on what can be the most exciting trip of your life!

To get started, complete the two exercises described below.

WATCH FOR SIGNS ALONG THE WAY

Road signs help drivers figure out how to get where they want to go. They provide clues about direction, road conditions, and safety. Your career road signs will provide clues about who you are, what you like, and what you do best. These clues can help you decide where to look for the career ideas that are best for you.

Complete the following statements to make them true for you. There are no right or wrong answers. Jot down the response that describes you best. Your answers will provide important clues about career paths you should explore.

Please Note: If this book does not belong to you, write your responses on a separate sheet of paper.

7

On my last report card, I got the best grade in _____.

On my last report card, I got the worst grade in _____.

I am happiest when _____.

Something I can do for hours without getting bored is _____.

Something that bores me out of my mind is _____.

My favorite class is _____.

My least favorite class is _____.

The one thing I'd like to accomplish with my life is _____.

My favorite thing to do after school is _.

My least favorite thing to do after school is _____.

Something I'm really good at is _____.

Something that is really tough for me to do is _____.

My favorite adult person is _____ because _____.

When I grow up _____.

The kinds of books I like to read are about _____.

The kinds of videos I like to watch are about _____.

GET SOME DIRECTION

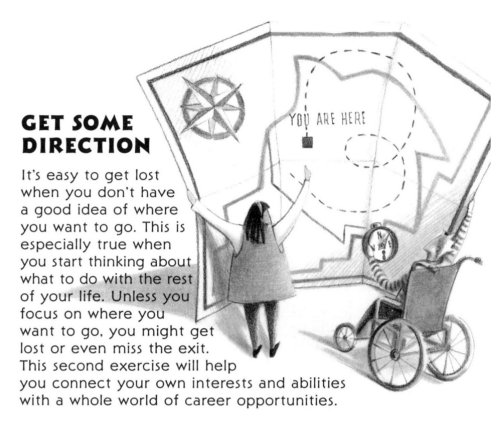

It's easy to get lost when you don't have a good idea of where you want to go. This is especially true when you start thinking about what to do with the rest of your life. Unless you focus on where you want to go, you might get lost or even miss the exit. This second exercise will help you connect your own interests and abilities with a whole world of career opportunities.

Mark the activities that you enjoy doing or would enjoy doing if you had the chance. Be picky. Don't mark ideas that you wish you would do, mark only those that you would really do. For instance, if the idea of skydiving sounds appealing, but you'd never do it because you are terrified of heights, don't mark it.

Please Note: If this book does not belong to you, write your responses on a separate sheet of paper.

- ❏ 1. Rescue a cat stuck in a tree
- ❏ 2. Visit the pet store every time you go to the mall
- ❏ 3. Paint a mural on the cafeteria wall
- ❏ 4. Send e-mail to a "pen pal" in another state
- ❏ 5. Survey your classmates to find out what they do after school
- ❏ 6. Run for student council
- ❏ 7. Try out for the school play
- ❏ 8. Dissect a frog and identify the different organs
- ❏ 9. Play baseball, soccer, football, or _____ (fill in your favorite sport)

❏ 10. Talk on the phone to just about anyone who will talk back

❏ 11. Try foods from all over the world—Thailand, Poland, Japan, etc.

❏ 12. Write poems about things that are happening in your life

❏ 13. Create a really scary haunted house to take your friends through on Halloween

❏ 14. Recycle all your family's trash

❏ 15. Bake a cake and decorate it for your best friend's birthday

❏ 16. Simulate an imaginary flight through space on your computer screen

❏ 17. Build model airplanes, boats, dollhouses, or anything from kits

❏ 18. Sell enough advertisements for the school yearbook to win a trip to Walt Disney World

❏ 19. Teach your friends a new dance routine

❏ 20. Watch the stars come out at night and see how many constellations you can find

❏ 21. Watch baseball, soccer, football, or _____ (fill in your favorite sport) on TV

❏ 22. Give a speech in front of the entire school

❏ 23. Plan the class field trip to Washington, D.C.

❏ 24. Read everything in sight, including the back of the cereal box

❏ 25. Figure out "who dunnit" in a mystery story

❏ 26. Take in stray or hurt animals

❏ 27. Make a poster announcing the school football game

❏ 28. Put together a multimedia show for a school assembly using music and lots of pictures and graphics

❏ 29. Think up a new way to make the lunch line move faster and explain it to the cafeteria staff

❏ 30. Invest your allowance in the stock market and keep track of how it does

❏ 31. Go to the ballet or opera every time you get the chance

❏ 32. Do experiments with a chemistry set

❏ 33. Keep score at your sister's Little League game

❏ 34. Use lots of funny voices when reading stories to children

❏ 35. Ride on airplanes, trains, boats—anything that moves

❏ 36. Interview the new exchange student for an article in the school newspaper

❏ 37. Build your own treehouse

❏ 38. Help clean up a waste site in your neighborhood

❏ 39. Visit an art museum and pick out your favorite painting

❏ 40. Make a chart on the computer to show how much soda students buy from the school vending machines each week

❏ 41. Keep track of how much your team earns to buy new uniforms

❏ 42. Play Monopoly® in an all-night championship challenge

❏ 43. Play an instrument in the school band or orchestra

❏ 44. Put together a 1,000-piece puzzle

❏ 45. Write stories about sports for the school newspaper

❏ 46. Listen to other people talk about their problems

❏ 47. Imagine yourself in exotic places

❏ 48. Hang around bookstores and libraries

❏ 49. Play harmless practical jokes on April Fools' Day

❑ 50. Join the 4-H club at your school
❑ 51. Take photographs at the school talent show
❑ 52. Create an imaginary city using a computer
❑ 53. Do 3-D puzzles
❑ 54. Make money by setting up your own business—paper route, lemonade stand, etc.
❑ 55. Keep track of the top 10 songs of the week
❑ 56. Train your dog to do tricks
❑ 57. Make play-by-play announcements at the school football game
❑ 58. Answer the phones during a telethon to raise money for orphans
❑ 59. Be an exchange student in another country
❑ 60. Write down all your secret thoughts and favorite sayings in a journal
❑ 61. Jump out of an airplane (with a parachute, of course)
❑ 62. Plant and grow a garden in your backyard (or windowsill)
❑ 63. Use a video camera to make your own movies
❑ 64. Spend your summer at a computer camp learning lots of new computer programs
❑ 65. Build bridges, skyscrapers, and other structures out of LEGO®s

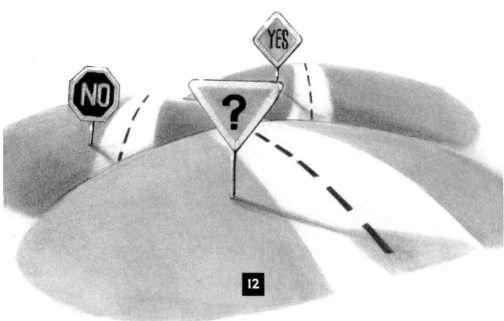

❏ 66. Get your friends together to help clean up your town after a hurricane
❏ 67. Plan a concert in the park for little kids
❏ 68. Collect different kinds of rocks
❏ 69. Help plan a sports tournament
❏ 70. Be DJ for the school dance
❏ 71. Learn how to fly a plane or sail a boat
❏ 72. Write funny captions for pictures in the school yearbook
❏ 73. Scuba dive to search for buried treasure
❏ 74. Recognize and name several different breeds of cats, dogs, and other animals
❏ 75. Sketch pictures of your friends
❏ 76. Answer your classmates' questions about how to use the computer
❏ 77. Draw a map showing how to get to your house from school
❏ 78. Pick out neat stuff to sell at the school store
❏ 79. Make up new words to your favorite songs
❏ 80. Take a hike and name the different kinds of trees, birds, or flowers
❏ 81. Referee intramural basketball games
❏ 82. Join the school debate team
❏ 83. Make a poster with postcards from all the places you went on your summer vacation
❏ 84. Write down stories that your grandparents tell you about when they were young

CALCULATE THE CLUES

Now is your chance to add it all up. Each of the 12 boxes on these pages contains an interest area that is common to both your world and the world of work. Follow these directions to discover your personal Skill Set:

1. Find all of the numbers that you checked on pages 9–13 in the boxes below and X them. Work your way all the way through number 84.
2. Go back and count the Xs marked for each interest area. Write that number in the space that says "total."
3. Find the interest area with the highest total and put a number one in the "Rank" blank of that box. Repeat this process for the next two highest scoring areas. Rank the second highest as number two and the third highest as number three.
4. If you have more than three strong areas, choose the three that are most important and interesting to you.

Remember: If this book does not belong to you, write your responses on a separate sheet of paper.

ADVENTURE	ANIMALS & NATURE	ART
❏ 1	❏ 2	❏ 3
❏ 13	❏ 14	❏ 15
❏ 25	❏ 26	❏ 27
❏ 37	❏ 38	❏ 39
❏ 49	❏ 50	❏ 51
❏ 61	❏ 62	❏ 63
❏ 73	❏ 74	❏ 75
Total: _____	Total: _____	Total: _____
Rank: _____	Rank: _____	Rank: _____

GET IN GEAR!

COMPUTERS

- ❑ 4
- ❑ 16
- ❑ 28
- ❑ 40
- ❑ 52
- ❑ 64
- ❑ 76
- Total: _____
- Rank: _____

MATH

- ❑ 5
- ❑ 17
- ❑ 29
- ❑ 41
- ❑ 53
- ❑ 65
- ❑ 77
- Total: _____
- Rank: _____

MONEY

- ❑ 6
- ❑ 18
- ❑ 30
- ❑ 42
- ❑ 54
- ❑ 66
- ❑ 78
- Total: _____
- Rank: _____

MUSIC/DANCE

- ❑ 7
- ❑ 19
- ❑ 31
- ❑ 43
- ❑ 55
- ❑ 67
- ❑ 79
- Total: _____
- Rank: _____

SCIENCE

- ❑ 8
- ❑ 20
- ❑ 32
- ❑ 44
- ❑ 56
- ❑ 68
- ❑ 80
- Total: _____
- Rank: _____

SPORTS

- ❑ 9
- ❑ 21
- ❑ 33
- ❑ 45
- ❑ 57
- ❑ 69
- ❑ 81
- Total: _____
- Rank: _____

TALKING

- ❑ 10
- ❑ 22
- ❑ 34
- ❑ 46
- ❑ 58
- ❑ 70
- ❑ 82
- Total: _____
- Rank: _____

TRAVEL

- ❑ 11
- ❑ 23
- ❑ 35
- ❑ 47
- ❑ 59
- ❑ 71
- ❑ 83
- Total: _____
- Rank: _____

WRITING

- ❑ 12
- ❑ 24
- ❑ 36
- ❑ 48
- ❑ 60
- ❑ 72
- ❑ 84
- Total: _____
- Rank: _____

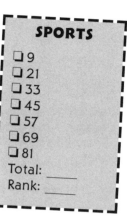
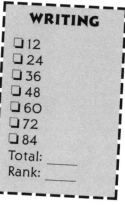
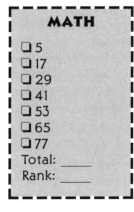
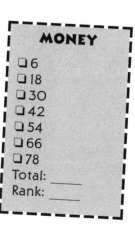
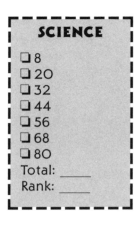

What are your top three interest areas? List them here (or on a separate piece of paper).

1. _____
2. _____
3. _____

WRITE YOUR RESPONSES ON A SEPARATE PIECE OF PAPER

This is your personal Skill Set and provides important clues about the kinds of work you're most likely to enjoy. Remember it and look for career ideas with a skill set that matches yours most closely.

TAKE A TRIP!

Cruise down the
career idea highway and
enjoy in-depth profiles of some of the interesting options in
this field. Keep in mind all that you've discovered about
yourself so far. Find the careers that match your own Skill
Set first. After that, keep on trucking through the other
ideas—exploration is the name of this game.

Don't be afraid to veer off the main "roads" a bit.
Everyone automatically seems to think singer or dancer
when you mention careers in the music industry. Sure, those
are great options for some people. But they aren't the only
options. Not by a long shot. For every one singer there are
dozens (and probably even hundreds or thousands if you

get right down to it) of other professionals supporting the music profession in creative and satisfying ways.

As you read about the following careers, imagine yourself doing each job and ask yourself the following questions:

☀ Would I like it?
☀ Would I be good at it?
☀ Is it the stuff my career dreams are made of?

If so, make a quick exit to explore what it involves. Try it out, check it out, and get acquainted!

Get that engine humming and off you go!

A NOTE ON WEBSITES

Internet sites tend to move around the Web a bit. If you have trouble finding a particular site mentioned in this section, use an Internet browser to find a specific website or type of information.

Arts Administrator

SHORTCUTS

SKILL SET

✔ MONEY

✔ MUSIC & DANCE

✔ WRITING

GO to an arts festival in your community and enjoy the many different kinds of artistic expression.

READ the entertainment section of the newspaper to find out about the local music and dance scene.

TRY volunteering to usher at a community theater or concert auditorium.

WHAT IS AN ARTS ADMINISTRATOR?

If the show must go on, it often starts long before the lights go down and performers take the stage. Concerts, musicals, dance performances, plays, and other kinds of theatrical productions often get their start in the office of an arts administrator. Arts administrators are important behind-the-scenes people who keep music and dance on the world's stages in theaters, auditoriums, museums, and schools. They accomplish this task in many ways.

It starts with the money. Budgets and finances are a big part of this job. It takes money, often vast amounts, to stage awe-inspiring productions. Not to mention the money it takes to maintain facilities, purchase equipment, pay staff, print programs, and all the other expenses associated with a steady stream of audience-pleasing shows. Arts administrators tend to look for funds in two ways. One is, obviously, ticket sales. Sold-out performances—every administrator's dream scenario—don't come without a lot of effort. It is important to put together performances people will pay to see. That's where an administrator assumes the role of artistic director by carefully and creatively building a winning roster of events. Next, the administrator has to make sure that people

know about each pro-
motion. Publicity, promo-
tions, and press
coverage are the
tools administra-
tors use to make
this happen.

But sold-out
performances
aren't enough.
Ticket sales alone
rarely cover all the
financial needs of an
organization. This fact
adds another dimension to
the arts administrator's job,
and it's called fund-raising. Fund-
raising involves finding businesses
that will sponsor various events in
what's called corporate partnerships. It
also involves writing proposals and
seeking grants from government agencies and charitable foundations that
fund arts programs. This can be a big
job, and it is often the sole responsibility of a special kind of administrator
called a development director.

Success in arts administration generally
requires several common factors. These factors
include a head for numbers, strong writing skills, and an ability to schmooze, or talk informally, with the bigwigs—
whether it's a performer, a corporate exec, or a patron. Some
of these skills can be obtained only with experience and on-
the-job training. Others come with an educational background strong in management and communications training.
Though not absolutely required, it can help to have a college
degree in business or administration with a strong emphasis
in the arts. Courses in theater, dance, music, or visual arts

provide knowledge and inspiration that often prove useful later on. Many colleges have programs in arts management that offer a good mix of business and artistic courses.

Administrators work just about any place where music and dance performances are found: in large and small theaters or dance companies, for cultural arts organizations and performing arts groups, in art galleries and museums, and for colleges, universities, and public schools. Nearly every major school district has an arts administrator on staff at least part-time to help integrate music, dance, visual arts, and other cultural experiences into the learning process for students of all ages.

Arts administrators play an important role in the entertainment industry. They bring stability to shoestring operations and continuity to major arts organizations. They handle the details that can make or break any type of musical or dance production. Administration is a career to consider for people who enjoy helping others succeed. It's also a career for those who wouldn't even want to imagine a world without music.

TRY IT OUT

PERFORMANCE OF THE MONTH

Wouldn't it be great if your school could host a big concert or dance performance every month? Maybe it's unlikely to happen in real life, but who says you can't dream a bit. Let's say that you've been chosen as arts administrator for your school. Your job is to fill 10 Friday nights—one for each month that school is in session—with great music and dance.

Here's what you do. First, take 10 sheets of paper and write the name of one month at the top of each sheet. Now for the talent. Scour the entertainment section of your local paper, look in magazines, and go on-line to websites featuring your favorite groups and find information. Clip or print out pictures of the groups you'd like to feature. Make sure to get a good mix of styles and performances.

Use the information you gather to make posters for promoting each event.

A CULTURAL ENCOUNTER

Arts administrators show up in the most incredible places, and their work benefits some of the worthiest organizations. For a showcase of several types of these organizations take some virtual tours on-line:

- Alvin Ailey American Dance Theater at http://alvinailey.org
- American Ballet Theater at http://www.abt.org
- Cooper-Hewitt National Design Museum at http://www.si.edu/ndm
- Meet the Composer, Inc. at http://www.meetthecomposer.org
- New York Metropolitan Opera House at http://www.metopera.org
- Smithsonian Institute at http://www.si.edu
- Washington Ballet at http://www.washingtonballet.org
- Women's Philharmonic at http://www.womensphil.org

Take special note of the programs they offer, the partners they mention, and any membership and donation opportunities they suggest. This is how they keep their organizations afloat.

HELP WANTED: ARTS ADMINISTRATOR

You're likely to find opportunities in unlikely places when you start looking for a job in arts administration. The following book provides a more in-depth look at some of the options:

Langley, Stephen, and James Abruzzo. *Jobs in Arts and Media Management: Where They Are and How to Get Them.* New York: Americans for the Arts, 1992.

PICK A WORTHY CAUSE

Now is the time to get some great experience as an arts administrator—even if you are just a kid. There is bound to be something you can do to help your school band or choral group. Maybe you can help organize a fund-raiser to help the band get new uniforms. Maybe you can pass out programs at the choir's next concert. Just let the music teachers know you are at their service, and they will most likely be glad to put you to work.

This same strategy may also work at your church or synagogue or at a community arts or theater group as well.

WHAT THE REAL PROS KNOW

Visit some of the following websites for a sampling of information and resources that arts administrators use in their work:

- ☀ Americans for the Arts at http://www.artsusa.org
- ☀ Art Jobs Online at http://www.artjob.org
- ☀ Arts Administration Websites at http://www.uno. edu/~arta
- ☀ Arts and Business at http://www.artsandbusiness.org
- ☀ Free Nonprofit Management Library at http://www. mapnp.org/library/index.html
- ☀ Nonprofit Toolkit at http://www.nptoolkit.org

CHECK IT OUT

American Arts Alliance
1319 F Street, Suite 500
Washington, D.C. 20004
http://www.artswire.org/~aaa

American Association of Museums
1225 I Street NW, Suite 200
Washington, D.C. 20005
http://www.aam-us.org

American Federation of the Arts
41 East 65th Street
New York, New York 10021
http://www.afaweb.org

Association of Arts
  Administration Educators
Teachers College

Columbia University
525 West 120th Street
New York, New York 10027
http://www.artsnet.org/aaae

National Association of
  Performing Arts Managers
137 East 30th Street, Suite 3B
New York, New York 10016
http://www.napama.org

National Endowment for
  the Arts
1100 Pennsylvania Avenue NW
Washington, D.C. 20506
http://arts.endow.gov

GET ACQUAINTED

Elizabeth Droessler,
Arts Administrator

CAREER PATH

CHILDHOOD ASPIRATION:
To be a dentist like her dad.

FIRST JOB: Working as an assistant in her dad's dental office.

CURRENT JOB: Senior administrator for arts education for Wake County Schools.

ABOUT FACE

There are a couple of things you need to know about Elizabeth Droessler. One is that music has always been a big part of her life. As a child she took piano lessons, played the flute and cello, had dance lessons, and was a cheerleader. Her mom was a school music teacher and played with the Fayetteville Symphony Orchestra. Her dad sang in a barbershop quartet.

The second thing you need to know about Droessler is that she'd always planned to be a dentist and even spent her first two years in college studying to become one. But then a weird thing happened.

One day Droessler was in the chemistry lab at school when it suddenly hit her (kind of like a brick) that dentistry was not the right choice for her. Without a second thought, she told her teacher she had to leave and went directly to the campus career planning office. There she said she thought she was in the wrong major. She was given a bunch of vocational interest tests and made a not-so-surprising discovery.

The test results indicated that the best career choices for Droessler involved jobs in which she could help people and jobs that involved the arts. That was that. Droessler transferred to a college that offered a degree in dance. Earning a master's degree in theater arts was next.

Now, well into a successful career in the arts, Droessler says she's only had one twinge of regret. That was when her father retired from his dental practice after spending 47 years as a dentist. For a minute there, she kind of wished she could take over the practice and continue the family tradition. Other than that, Droessler is glad she followed her heart.

ARTS FOR ALL

Droessler's first job out of college involved a short stint incorporating creative movement and drama into the curriculum for three elementary schools. She then spent three years teaching dance and technical theater at a special arts-focused middle school. From there, she was chosen to help lead the school district's arts education department.

Now she is the senior administrator of the program and is responsible for supervising the 425 teachers who teach band, strings, general music, choral music, visual arts, dance, and theater arts in the county's elementary, middle, and high schools.

It is a huge job. Her responsibilities are as varied as coordinating county-wide art shows, organizing opportunities for all the county's third-graders to visit an art museum, budgeting enough money to pay for repairs for the county's band and string instruments, helping choreograph high school musicals, and training new teachers.

She says the job is especially fun because it lets her "think outside the box." She likes introducing teachers and students to rules that are unique to arts programs. For instance, a favorite rule is "you must be creative at all times." Another one is "you can talk only about art projects during class."

NOT JUST A DAY JOB

The arts are not just the focus of Droessler's professional life. They often spill over into her personal life as well. She and her husband, Chris, run the Barnabas Company on the weekends and during school holidays. They describe the company as an "expensive hobby" and labor of love that involves providing sound and lighting design for musicians and performers whom they care about. One of Droessler's favorite clients is the African American Dance Ensemble. She's traveled all over the country with this group and never tires of using lights to create a mood onstage that sparks an audience's imagination. Every once in a while, she even gets to dance with the troupe!

Droessler and her husband share their artistic talents in another way as leaders of a Boy Scout Explorer post that focuses on technical theater. Their post offers career exploration opportunities to both male and female high school students with an interest in the behind-the-scenes aspects of theater work. There are Explorer posts for all kinds of careers including law enforcement, health care, and television production. Droessler urges students to contact their state Boy Scout organization for information about this wonderful program.

A PERFECT FIT

Given all her experience in the arts, Droessler has learned an important lesson that she wants you to know. She says that you don't have to be the one taking a bow onstage to have a great future in arts. There are so many opportunities for people to support the arts—backstage, behind-the-scenes, nurturing a new generation of artists, and more. Droessler says that you don't have to limit yourself to the obvious: dancer, singer, actor. Follow your heart, go with your strengths, and see where they take you. Like Droessler, you just may end up right where you belong!

Booking Agent

WHAT IS A BOOKING AGENT?

Making music is one thing. Making money for making music is another thing altogether. That's where booking agents come in. A booking agent has two main jobs. First is finding talent, or performers to represent. Second is finding places for those performers to perform for pay. Performances can include anything from a standing-room-only concert in a major concert hall or auditorium to an artist-in-residence program at a school like yours. Other possibilities include hotels, clubs, amusement parks, dinner playhouses, festivals, and anywhere else people go to be entertained. Sometimes a booking agent is responsible for finding commercials, television programs, or major theater productions for their clients to perform in as well.

It's easy to make the mistake of assuming that agents only work in places such as Hollywood or New York. Not true. There are booking agencies in nearly every city. Sure, there's a booking agent scheduling the big-name stars on the international tours and in special performances. But there are a lot more agents who work with talented local performers in places all over the country.

Booking agents tend to work with a variety of clients and specialize in one or more ways. Some may work strictly with

dancers, while others work with opera singers, rock groups, or family entertainers. For big-name talent, agents may spend as much or more time responding to requests for performances as they do trying to find them. Their focus is on choosing the best ways to showcase their client's talent. Agents working with local talent may spend time schmoozing at booking conferences, art councils, and other forums to get their client's schedule filled with interesting (and lucrative) performance dates.

Either way, booking agents spend a good portion of any day on the phone making arrangements and staying on top of those all-important details. Finding places to perform is only the first step. Then there are contracts to negotiate, travel arrangements to be made, all kinds of coordination and logistics to deal with—details, details, details. Let a detail or two fall through the cracks and havoc is bound to ensue. Even though performers must pay their booking agents a percentage of their fees (anywhere from 10 to 20 percent), good agents are worth their weight in gold. With booking agents handling all the details, performers can concentrate on performing.

There are really only two requirements for becoming a booking agent. First, is finding talent to represent. Second, is obtaining any required licenses from the state where the talent will conduct business. The license is the easy part. Finding the right mix of talent to book is a certain talent in itself.

Therefore, good training, experience, and the right contacts are extremely important in this field. It is possible to become a booking agent without going to college. There are seminars and workshops to attend and books to read that can provide the nuts and bolts information you need to become a booking agent. However, the do-it-yourself route won't necessarily bring you the contacts you need to get started. Making the right connections often comes from working with an established talent agency first. And working in some of the best agencies often requires having a college degree.

As in all career paths, different educational routes work for different people. Weigh your options carefully. However, the college route may open the most doors for an aspiring booking agent—unless, of course, it's looking like your best friend has enough musical talent to take you both to the big time.

However, the right degree from a good college can only help your chances as you work your way up through the ranks. Consider pursuing a degree in music management, business management, or public relations. These types of programs offer courses that equip booking agents with the communication skills and business savvy necessary to manage someone else's career.

Other career options along the same vein as booking agent include:

Concert promoters do much of the planning and even some of the funding that goes into hosting a concert or special performance. They generally make decisions concerning all the who, what, when, where questions associated with a concert. Who will perform? Where will the concert be held? What dates? How will the event be publicized? And, certainly a big concern, how will this event be profitable?

Personal managers add another twist to the booking agent career track. They handle the business side of a performer's career and help guide their clients toward the best opportunities. The right personal manager can often mean the difference between mediocre and mega success for all kinds of performers.

Publicists get the word out about upcoming performances through advertisements, press releases, posters, and other means. Whenever appropriate and possible, publicists also try to schedule radio, newspaper, and television interviews for their artists. It's never fun to throw a party—or a concert—and have no one show up! Filling seats and selling tickets are what publicists aim for in all their work.

These options all provide a front-row seat to exciting aspects of the entertainment business. Booking agents might not share the limelight with their clients, but they do share their success. That's what makes this job so much fun.

TRY IT OUT

TALK OF THE TRADE

The telephone is *the* tool of the trade for booking agents. They use phones to book performances, to stay in touch with clients, to negotiate contracts, and so on. Taking different time zones into account, a booking agent scheduling an international tour could literally stay on the phone for 24 hours a day!

Whether 24/7 or just 9 to 5, good phone habits are a must-have skill for booking agents. Now is as good a time as any to work on yours so here are some activities to try.

- ☀ Pick a greeting that sounds reasonably polite, and surprise your family and friends by answering the phone that way every day for a week. Watch out—it could be habit forming!
- ☀ Ask your friend to help you out by pretending to be the owner of a trendy new club in town. You take on the role of booking agent for your favorite music

group. Call your friend and try to convince him or her to book your client for the grand opening of the club. Be prepared for all their questions! Know before you dial why your client would be the best choice for the job.

☼ Keeping track of phone calls is almost as important as making them in the booking business. Keep a small notebook next to the phone in your house for a couple days. Use it to keep a phone log noting every time the phone rings, who the call is from, who the call is for, and any message that you might need to remember.

ON THE ROAD

Pretend you are a booking agent representing a promising new musician. Pick a style of music—jazz, alternative, or rock—and give the group a name. Now go on-line to http://www.festivalfinder.com or http://www.musical.com and find some appropriate music festivals where your client might be hired to work.

Next go on-line to http://www.musiciansguide.com. Here you can search a city-by-city directory of clubs, music stores, radio stations, and local media sources to find other ways for your artist to make the most of his or her time in a certain place. Are there other clubs nearby where you might book your client? What newspapers and radio stations can you contact about interviewing your client to get some media coverage while you are there? Maybe a music store would like to host a CD-signing event with your artist? Booking agents get paid to think through all the possibilities. Another good source of on-line information is http://www.musiciansatlas.com.

If you don't have access to a computer, make up a schedule of festivals, concerts, and clubs where you've booked your "virtual" client, or use books such as *The Musicians Guide to Touring and Promotion* (New York: Billboard Books, 2000) or *The Musician's Atlas* (Montclair, N.J.: Music Resource Group, 2000). List the dates, the locations, and the fees.

Double-check to make sure that you haven't arranged for your client to be in two places at the same time and look at a map to make sure the tour route is reasonable. For example, can your client possibly make the drive from a concert in Santa Barbara, California, held on Tuesday to a festival in Fort Lauderdale, Florida, on Wednesday? Those little details will get you every time!

IN THE KNOW AND UP TO DATE

Booking agents everywhere rely on information found in the trade papers to keep them informed about what's going on in the industry. You'll find the inside scoop in publications such as *Variety, Backstage, Billboard,* and *Hollywood Reporter* at your local newsstand.

Or go on-line and visit these websites:

- *Variety* at http://www.variety.com
- *Backstage* at http://www.backstage.com
- *Billboard* at http://www.billboard.com
- *Hollywood Reporter* at http://www. hollywoodreporter. com

While you're at it, see if you can identify at least five of the current hottest stars. Compare what each of the publications has to say about these artists.

CHECK IT OUT

American Federation of Musicians
1501 Broadway, Suite 600
New York, New York 10036
http://www.afm.org

American Guild of Musical Artists
1727 Broadway
New York, New York 10019
http://www.agmanatl.com

Association of Performing Arts Presenters
1112 Sixteenth Street NW, Suite 400
Washington, D.C. 20036
http://www.artspresenters.org

Association of Talent Agents
9255 Sunset Boulevard, Suite 930
Los Angeles, California 90069
http://www.agentassociation.com

Music and Entertainment Industry Educators Association
http://www.meiea.org

Music and Entertainment Industry Students Association
http://www.meisa.org

National Association of Performing Arts Managers and Agents
459 Columbus Avenue, Suite 133
New York, New York 20035
http://www.napama.org

National Conference of Personal Managers
210 East 51st Street
New York, New York 10022
http://www.cybershowbiz.com/ncopm

GET ACQUAINTED

Jeri Goldstein, Booking Agent

CAREER PATH

CHILDHOOD ASPIRATION: To be an artist.

FIRST JOB: Camp counselor.

CURRENT JOB: Music industry consultant, author, and publisher.

ONE THING LED TO ANOTHER

Jeri Goldstein went to college intending to become an art therapist. She even used her artistic skills to help pay her way through school. But, as is often the case for even the most well-intentioned career planner, opportunities led her elsewhere.

It all started in junior college when Goldstein got a job designing posters for the student activities office to advertise campus events such as concerts, festivals, and special lectures.

The student activities director liked Goldstein's work, and before long Goldstein's duties expanded. Soon Goldstein was researching various types of talent to book for student events, interacting with booking agents, and helping produce different kinds of events.

Moving on to another college, Goldstein's experience helped her clinch a job as manager of the campus coffeehouse. The coffeehouse was a cool place for students to hang out, have a snack, and listen to some good music. One of Goldstein's jobs was to find and schedule interesting performers to keep things hopping at the coffeehouse. It was a task that Goldstein was very good at.

Organized person that she is, Goldstein not only took care of booking these groups for her coffeehouse, she also found gigs for them at other nearby colleges to help defray their traveling costs. One thing led to another, and some of the groups asked her to help them find bookings in other places as well. From those innocent beginnings, a long and very successful career began.

DON'T GIVE UP YOUR DAY JOB

Nice as it would be to say that Goldstein's business started making millions of dollars overnight, that's not how it happened. Instead, Goldstein's story is one of step-by-step growth, a career path with all kinds of interesting twists and turns.

Yes, she graduated from college already handling bookings for several folk, country, and bluegrass groups. But the groups were just starting out, their performance fees weren't exactly staggering, and Goldstein couldn't earn enough to support herself. No problem. She was young. She had a degree and plenty of skills to boot. She would subsidize her income with a "real" job for the first few years. That was a smart move since these jobs were all related to the entertainment industry: commercial television production engineer, commercial country radio DJ, graphic artist, and photographer. At one point, Goldstein was booking acts while working as a radio DJ during the day and working as sound engineer for a local NBC affiliate at night.

THE WORLD'S A STAGE

As Goldstein's experience and contacts grew, so did her business. At first, she only handled bookings in the northeastern states. Then, region by region, she started growing her business—first booking tours in the Midwest, then moving on to include all 50 states, and, eventually, planning worldwide tours for some of her clients.

Territory isn't the only way that Goldstein's business grew. Her responsibilities to her clients soon grew well beyond booking to include promotion, management, and publishing.

SOME DAYS ARE LIKE THAT

Ask Goldstein what she likes least about being a booking agent, and she'll say the dry spells. Trudging through an entire day without a single booking is no fun. But Goldstein has learned to hang in there until her client's schedules are full of good dates.

On the other hand, Goldstein says the best part of the job is watching unknown artists become well-recognized talents. Their success is her success, and it's one of the best perks of this job.

THE BOOK ON BOOKING

You can benefit from Goldstein's 20-plus years in the entertainment business by reading her book, *How to Be Your Own Booking Agent: A Performing Artist's Guide to a Successful Touring Career* (Charlottesville, Va.: The New Music Times, Inc., 2000).

Choir Director

WHAT IS A CHOIR DIRECTOR?

Take a piece of music, add several singers with talents of varying degrees, throw in a piano and organ with people to play them, and put them all together in a room with someone waving a wand. What have you got? A choir. That person waving the wand is the choir director. His or her job is to take that hodgepodge of musicians and music and put it all together in perfect harmony.

Many choir directors work for churches or synagogues. Others work in schools, colleges, universities, or community arts organizations. Whether leading hymns or operas, most choir directors have one thing in common: volunteers. More often than not, choirs are made up of people who love music but have busy lives full of work, family, and other responsibilities. That leaves limited amounts of time available for rehearsals and performances. And this means that a choir director must be prepared for every rehearsal.

Before rehearsals, choir directors have done their homework and lots of it. They've carefully chosen musical selections that fit the needs of the congregation as well as the abilities of the choir. They've listened to recordings of the musical selections and made any necessary adjustments to their arrangements. They've order ample supplies of music books so that each choir member has a copy. They practice each part of the selection and rehearse conducting the piece. Yes, there's a lot more to the job of choir director than meets the eye.

In a church setting, a choir director may also be responsible for an entire music program. That may include planning the sequence of songs for congregational singing for one or more services each week, working with soloists and other special music groups, organizing plays and musical productions, and leading children's and youth choirs. Oh, and don't forget coordinating all this with the pianist, church orchestra, and other church ministers. All this is typical of a week's work, but it doesn't include planning special events such as weddings, funerals, and church celebrations that occur frequently in the life of any congregation.

In Judaism, a choir director is called a cantor and holds an esteemed place in a temple or synagogue. A cantor uses music to help clarify prayers and religious study. He or she may also

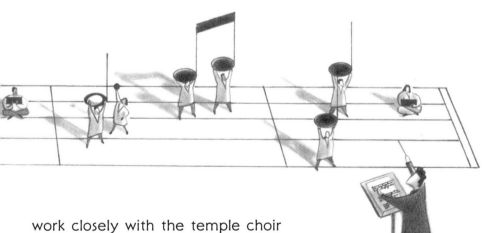

work closely with the temple choir and teach music to help children prepare for special ceremonies. Once again, the work involves much more than is seen during a typical worship service.

Likewise, duties can also expand for other types of choir directors. Some college choirs travel around the country or even the world as representatives of their school. Others perform at a variety of school and community functions as well as in state and national competitions. Much of the preparation and planning for these activities falls to the choir director.

Along similar lines is another type of musical career choice—that of conductor. Conductors are to orchestras what choir directors are to choirs. Conductors are most often associated with symphony or philharmonic orchestras found in major cultural centers and in many larger cities.

All of these careers require a solid musical background, ability to sight-read music, an understanding of music theory and technique, and a proficiency in playing at least one instrument. This type of knowledge generally comes from college-level study in music and as much firsthand experience in musical performance as possible.

Whether choir director, cantor, or conductor, this type of profession offers a rare opportunity to share the joy of music in personally meaningful ways. The work is all about using music to touch a certain corner of the world—to inspire, to comfort, to celebrate.

TRY IT OUT

MUSICAL ABCS

Choir directors have to know how to read music in order to do their jobs. You can learn the basics on-line at these web-sites:

- ☿ Learn2 Read Music at http://www.learn2.com/O9/O917/O917.asp
- ☿ Music Central at http://www.geocities.com/SunsetStrip/Club/3494/reading.htm.
- ☿ Introduction to Reading Music at http://www.datadragon.com/education/reading

Choir Director

MUSICAL FUN AND GAMES
Learn a little and have some fun at some of these goofy websites:

- ✸ Mr. Note's Gameland at http://www.talenz.com/ MusicEd/MrNoteGameland/MrNoteGameland.mv.
- ✸ Play Composer Concentration at http://www. classicalmusic.about.com/musicperform/ classicalmusic/library/games/con.../blcomposer.htm.
- ✸ Play a round (or two) of Classical Music Trivia at http://gamecenter.about.com/trivia/classicalmusic/ plugin.htm.
- ✸ Who needs an instrument when you've got a Touch-Tone phone? Play your own telephone symphony at http://www.laffinow.com/humor/touch_to.htm.

ROLE REHEARSALS
The choir director at your church or synagogue has just called in sick, and you've been asked to fill it. Take your pick of selecting music for the wedding, the funeral, the graduation ceremony, the Mother's Day celebration, or the teen service—all events scheduled for this week. What songs can you find that help set the tone for each service? Use a church hymnal or your own CD collection to come up with a plan that includes a selection for the choir as well as a couple of songs for the audience to sing together.

MUSIC BOOKS
Here are two good choices for reading about music basics:

Ardly, Neil, and Paul Ruders. *A Young Person's Guide to Music.* New York: DK Publishing, 1995.
Ganeri, Anita, and Ben Kingsley. *The Young Person's Guide to the Orchestra.* New York: Harcourt Brace, 1996.

AN ORCHESTRA OF WEBSITES

The Internet can be the instrument of choice for learning more about choirs and orchestras. Here are some website "notes" to strike for behind-the-curtain looks at some famous symphonies:

- ☺ Dallas Symphony Orchestra at http://www.dsokids.com
- ☺ New York Philharmonic Kidzone at http://www.nyphilkids.org

To find out how musical instruments work visit http://www.library.thinkquest.org/3656/html/how.htm.

TEACH THE WORLD TO SING

Find links to more than 1,600 choir sites from all over the world at http://www.choralnet.org and information about all things related to bands and orchestras at the Ensemble website at http://www.ensemble.org.

CHECK IT OUT

American Choral Directors
Association
502 SW 38th Street
Lawton, Oklahoma 73505
http://www.acdaonline.org

American Symphony Orchestra
League
33 West 60th Street, 5th Floor
New York, New York 10023
http://www.symphony.org

Cantors Assembly
Jewish Theological Seminary
3080 Broadway, Suite 613
New York, New York 10027
http://www.cantors.org

Choristers Guild
2834 West Kingsley Road
Garland, Texas 75041
http://www.choristersguild.com

Conductors Guild
103 South High Street,
Suite 6
West Chester, Pennsylvania
19382

GET ACQUAINTED

Paul T. Kwami, Choir Director

CAREER PATH

CHILDHOOD ASPIRATION: To be a spy.

FIRST JOB: Teacher at a middle school in Ghana.

CURRENT JOB: Professor at Fisk University and director of Jubilee Singers.

A FAMILY TRADITION

Paul T. Kwami was born and raised in Ghana where his father was an accomplished musician, working as a composer, church organist, choir conductor, and music teacher. Even though Kwami was surrounded by music as a child, he did not consider music as something he wanted to do for a living at first. He was more interested in taking things apart and putting them back together, trying to figure out how cars work, and fixing things around the house. As a boy, he didn't see the worth of music as a profession.

After graduating from high school, he was grateful to be accepted into one of only three universities in Ghana, and there he studied to become a teacher. While still in college, he worked as an assistant to the university's organist and as a high school choral music teacher.

When he completed the college program, he was hired to teach all subjects in a middle school. It took only one year for him to realize that he didn't like teaching everything. He wanted to focus on a subject he really cared about so that he could prepare better and have a greater impact on his students.

That's when he realized that following in his father's footsteps wasn't such a bad idea after all. He enrolled in the

National Academy of Music, a four-year college in Ghana that trains teachers of music. After graduating, he was hired to teach piano, the male voice choir, theory of music, and sight singing at the academy.

A LONG WAY FROM HOME

Curiosity got the best of Kwami after a few years of teaching. He wanted to learn more about the American music system, which he understood to be quite different from what he had learned in Ghana (a former British colony).

A missionary he met in Ghana suggested that Kwami attend Fisk University, which is exactly what he did next. Kwami said that there were a few cultural surprises awaiting him when he arrived in Nashville, Tennessee, to attend classes. For one thing, the other students laughed at his accent, so it took him awhile to feel comfortable asking questions in his classes. For another thing, the food and weather were so much different in the United States than they were at home. He was also surprised to discover that many students didn't take college quite as seriously as they did back in Ghana.

After some time, he settled in and enjoyed earning a bachelor's degree at Fisk. Then he took off for Michigan where he earned a master's degree at Western Michigan University.

With his education completed (at least for the time being), Kwami returned to Nashville where he worked in the choral department of a sheet music store. Then he was invited to take over as temporary director of Fisk's legendary Jubilee Singers for a semester. He later applied and was accepted as official director of the group as well as a teacher of several music courses. Now he is also chairman of the music department as well.

A CULTURAL LINK

The Jubilee Singers group has a long and proud history. Established in 1871, all but two of the original singers had been slaves. The group was essentially formed as a last-ditch effort to raise funds for the struggling Fisk University, a school established for freed slaves just six months after the

Civil War ended. Given the cultural climate at the time, a singing group featuring freed slaves singing "slave songs" was a bold idea. The original singers endured some tough times and more than a few tense moments on stage before becoming a widely acclaimed group. They went on to sing for President Ulysses Grant at the White House and throughout the United States and Europe.

Kwami considers it a great honor now to be the director of the Jubilee Singers. The group continues the tradition of singing Negro spirituals a cappella (without musical instruments). Kwami believes that the group not only represents Fisk University but the entire nation as they share an important part of America's cultural expression with audiences everywhere. His dream is to have the group someday perform in his homeland of Ghana, a place where many of the songs they sing originated. He sees it as a way to bring the music full circle and as a wonderful cultural experience for the students and audiences alike.

ALL IN A DAY'S WORK

Kwami says that an important part of his job as director of the Jubilee Singers is to maintain the high standards of music the group is known for. He spends a lot of time researching Negro spirituals to find selections that showcase the best of this style of music. He tries to include a variety of songs and always includes some very simple songs that children can learn and understand. Passing on a musical legacy is what this group has always stood for.

Kwami now understands that his boyhood reluctance to go into music is not at all unusual. Sometimes children have big ideas of wanting to make lots of money and such. However, Kwami believes that the satisfaction he finds in his work is worth much more than money can buy.

You can find out more about Kwami's work at Fisk University at http://www.fisk.edu/jubilee/general_information.htm. For a look at the history of the Jubilee Singers go to http://www.pbs.org/wgbh/amex/singers.

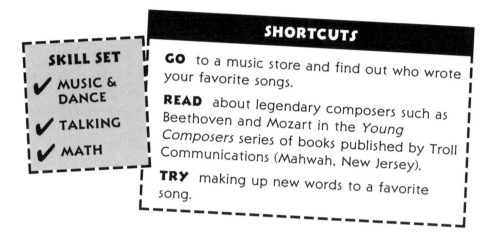

Composer

SHORTCUTS

SKILL SET

✔ MUSIC & DANCE

✔ TALKING

✔ MATH

GO to a music store and find out who wrote your favorite songs.

READ about legendary composers such as Beethoven and Mozart in the *Young Composers* series of books published by Troll Communications (Mahwah, New Jersey).

TRY making up new words to a favorite song.

WHAT IS A COMPOSER?

When you say "composer," the first thing that comes to mind for many people is Mozart, Bach or one of the other creators of timeless classical music. Some think of symphonies or great orchestras. Others may think of operas or rip-roaring Broadway musicals. And while all these responses would be 100 percent correct, they tell only part of the story. Composers and songwriters are the creative minds behind every song played on the radio, all the jingles included in advertisements, the sound tracks that accompany movies and TV shows, and all your favorite CDs.

It doesn't really matter if the results are grand and lofty or just plain goofy, the process for composing music and writing lyrics (the words to a song) is much the same. Forget any silly notions about sudden inspiration—words and melodies to a string of top-ten hits striking like a bolt of lightning. Success as a composer rarely comes that way. Writing songs is really hard work.

Working as a composer starts with musical talent. Composers of television, film, and orchestral music must know how to read music. They must understand the various roles that different instruments play in each composition—

whether it's a full-fledged orchestra or a fiddle and some drums. They must have something to say in their music, but even more important, they must know how to say it in a way that others want to hear. Other skills that come in handy include creativity, a good memory, an eye for details, an ear for music, self-discipline, and lots of persistence.

Since songwriting can be such a competitive endeavor, it doesn't hurt to also have thick skin. That's the only way to be prepared to deal with the inevitable rejection and disappointment that comes to even the most talented composers.

If you have the musical gift of a Mozart, no one is going to stand in your way if you don't have a college degree. Write good music, get someone to perform and produce it, and you are a composer. However, many musicians find that the training and discipline they receive by working toward a college degree helps refine their talent and further their careers. Common courses of study include performing arts, music composition, music history, or music performance. Some colleges offer programs tailored especially for songwriters.

In addition to the option of obtaining a formal college education, there are also a number of intensive songwriting workshops and seminars that many composers and songwriters find helpful. These are especially available in major music centers such as Los Angeles, New York, and Nashville.

Songwriters and composers find work in a variety of ways. Probably the vast majority are freelancers who work on their music in addition to holding down other jobs. Some are employed by orchestras or opera houses while others teach in universities. Quite a few composers and songwriters work full-time on staff for record labels, music publishers, movie studios, and other types of entertainment-related businesses.

Make no mistake, composing music and writing songs is not an easy way to make a living. It is generally best left to those who can't think of anything they'd rather be doing. For those people, the joy of creating wonderful music is compensation enough while they wait for their lucky break.

TRY IT OUT

MEET THE COMPOSER

Thanks to the Internet, you can go back in time and meet some of the world's great composers such as Beethoven, Mozart, Schubert, and Sousa. Find out all about these remarkable people and others at these websites:

- Mrs. Carrier's Middle School Music Page at http://users. massed.net/~carrier
- Catalogue of Classical Composers at http://www. uoregon.edu/~lincicum/comp.html
- Essentials of Music at http://www. essentialsofmusic.com
- Worldwide Internet Music Resources at http://www. music.indiana.edu/music_resources/composer.html

Choose a favorite and visit several websites to find out all you can about them.

WRITE A PRETTY DITTY

Songs are often poetry set to music. Perhaps you've noticed that the words in poems often rhyme. Try writing the lyrics to a song with rhyming words. The song can be about your pet, a good friend, something that you think about a lot, or something completely zany. If you get stuck thinking up words that rhyme, go on-line for help to the Online Rhyming Dictionary at http://www.rhyme.lycos.com. More songwriting ideas can be found at the Lyrical Line at http://www.lyricalline.com.

For some good songwriting advice and resources also visit

- ☼ The Songwriter's Connection at http://www. journeypublishing.com
- ☼ The Lyricists website at http://www.lyricist.com
- ☼ Just Plain Folks Songwriting/Musician Networking Organization at http://www.jpfolks.com/home.html
- ☼ The Solo Performer at http://www.soloperformer.com/ careers/starting.html

THE COMPOSER IS IN

Now that you've got the words to a new song, make up a tune to go with it. If you play an instrument, use it to put your words to music. If not, the Internet is, once again, the place to be. Go to the Music Emporium at http://library.thinkquest.org/3656/html/2how.htm where you can compose your own music. First, explore the "how they work" section to decide which instruments you want to include. Strings, woodwinds, brass, and percussion are the options. Then click on the "compose your own music" icon and put your personal orchestra to work.

If you'd rather keep things simple and use only a keyboard, head for the nearest piano or go on-line to a virtual keyboard at http://www.xmission.com/~mgm/misc/keyboard.html.

THE MUSE'S MUSE

According to Greek mythology, The muses were the nine Greek goddesses who presided over the arts. Their presence brought inspiration to artists. Now when someone refers to a muse, they are talking about the inspiration that motivates a poet, artist, or thinker. As a budding songwriter or composer, you may find inspiration and ideas at a really cool website called the Muse's Muse. It's located at http://www.muses-muse.com. Take a tour and see what you think.

Opportunities for further musings about music can be found in books such as:

Stewart, Dave. *Inside the Music: The Musician's Guide to Composition, Improvisation and the Mechanics of Music.* San Francisco: Miller Freeman Books, 1999.

A DAY AT THE OPERA

OK, so it's not exactly hip-hop, but opera is really good for you (kind of like spinach for the musician). It often showcases brilliant musical composition, and you can learn a lot by listening to the stories that operas tell with music. So if you ever get the chance to see an opera performance in person, do it—even if it's not your favorite style of music.

Until then, enjoy a cyber musical experience at some of the world's most famous opera houses. Here are some websites to conduct a musical grand tour:

☼ New York City Opera at http://www.nycopera.com
☼ The Royal Opera House at http://www.royalopera.org
☼ San Diego Opera House at http://www.sdopera.com
☼ San Francisco Opera at http://www.sfopera.com
☼ Washington Opera at http://www.dc-opera.org

Several of these websites include some fun educational activities as well as good information. Take the time to browse and learn.

CHECK IT OUT

American Composers Alliance
170 West 75th Street
New York, New York 10023
http://www.composers.com

American Composers Forum
332 Minnesota Street, Suite East 145
St. Paul, Minnesota 55101
http://www.composersforum.org

American Music Center
30 West 26th Street, Suite 1001
New York, New York 10010
http://www.amc.net

American Society of Composers, Authors, and Publishers
One Lincoln Plaza
New York, New York 10023
http://www.ascap.com

American Society of Music Arrangers and Composers
P.O. Box 17840
Encino, California 91416
http://www.asmac.org

BMI
10 Music Square East
Nashville, Tennessee 37203
http://www.bmi.com

League of Composers
P.O. Box 250281
Columbia University Station
New York, New York 10025
http://www.thegroovelab.com/composers

Nashville Songwriters Association International
15 Music Square West
Nashville, Tennessee 37203
http://www.nashvillesongwriters.com

National Academy of Popular Music
330 West 58ᵗʰ Street, Suite 411
New York, New York 10019
http://www.songwritershalloffame.org/napm/index.html

National Association of Composers
P.O. Box 49652
Barrington Station
Los Angeles, California 90049
http://www.music-usa.org/nacusa

Society of Composers and Lyricists
400 South Beverly Drive, Suite 214
Beverly Hills, California 90212
http://www.filmscore.org

Songwriters Guild of America
1500 Harbor Boulevard
Weehawken, New Jersey 07087
http://www.songwriters.org

GET ACQUAINTED

Jason Blume, Songwriter

Jason Blume with
Britney Spears

CAREER PATH

CHILDHOOD ASPIRATION: To be a recording artist.

FIRST JOB: Was always doing something to earn a few extra bucks as a kid, including mowing lawns and pet sitting.

CURRENT JOB: Staff songwriter for Zomba Music, author, and songwriting teacher.

NO OTHER CHOICE

Jason Blume wrote his first song when he was 12 and dreamed of becoming a performer who wrote his own songs. His musical heroes included Cat Stevens, Joni Mitchell, Elton John, and the Beatles.

Blume pursued music throughout his school years, but when it came time to go to college he listened to his parents' advice. Concerned that there was no future for their son in music, Blume's parents urged him to pursue something he could "fall back on" just in case. So Blume studied psychology instead of music. He graduated from college fully expecting to spend the rest of his career working in a psychiatric hospital.

About a year and a half into this career, Blume realized he just couldn't do it. His heart wasn't in it. He had to give a career in music a shot.

Blume quit his job, loaded up his car with everything he owned, filled his wallet with the only money he had (a whopping $400), and headed cross-country to Los Angeles. His plan was to write and perform his own songs, and he fully believed that he would be famous within a year.

Never mind that he was so poor that he could only afford to rent one room and had to share a bathroom with 12 other people! Never mind that there were times he was so broke that all he could afford to eat was a 12-cent can of kitty tuna (yes, it's *supposed* to be for cats), but he was following his dream. And Blume recalls those early years as some of the happiest in his life.

THE LONG HAUL

Needless to say, fame and fortune did not come knocking on Blume's door within a year. But Blume did not give up. He knew he had a lot to learn about the music industry, so he set about learning all he could in some very clever ways.

First of all, Blume enrolled in every workshop for songwriters that he could find. He says that until then he had just been writing the songs that flowed from his heart. In these workshops, he learned the techniques and acquired the tools to write for an audience. Blume says that a songwriter's main job is to write songs that give people the words they wish they could say and the melodies they want to hear and sing.

Blume also used his need to earn a living to further his music education. Living in Los Angeles, Blume found plenty of opportunity to work right in the middle of the entertainment industry. He started out typing and filing for a public relations firm that managed a number of big stars and worked his way up to director of public relations. He worked as receptionist for a film company and ended up writing music for their films. Then he got a job working in the country music promotion department at a major record label. He started out as an assistant to the assistant and eventually moved into the pop A&R (artist and repertoire) department where part of his job was to help find songs for the label's artists to sing and new talent to sign to the label. He was right where he needed to be—learning the ins and outs of the business and making incredible connections with famous artists such as Naomi and Wynona Judd, Kenny Rogers, Alabama, Diana Ross, and Barry Manilow.

Blume credits two things for his eventual success: his belief that he would someday make it and his willingness to go to any length to make it happen. He never sat back and waited for success to come to him. Instead, he relentlessly pursued it.

TWO STEPS FORWARD, ONE STEP BACK

After about 10 years in Los Angeles, three big things happened that turned Blume's career around. One is that he realized that he was not going to make it as a performing artist. It was a sad realization, but it freed him to pour everything into writing songs for other performers. Two is that Blume entered an international songwriting contest and won the right to represent the United States. The contest pitted his work against that of songwriters from 10 other countries. Blume admits he fared badly in the end; however, just having been chosen to compete was enough to move Blume up a notch as a songwriter.

Which leads to the third big event. A well-known song-writer named Bryan Cummings agreed to collaborate with Blume on a song he was writing. Blume thought it would be perfect for the Judds and submitted it to a publisher he had met through his work at the record company. The publisher thought it had potential but needed more work. Blume and Cummings ended up rewriting the song seven times before it made the cut.

Within 24 hours of being accepted by the publisher, the song was recorded by a new artist named Darlene Austin. The song made the Billboard top 100 list almost immediately. It was Blume's first big break.

AIMING HIGH

With a song on the charts, Blume used his newfound "clout" to arrange to work with a songwriter who had written several country hits. Blume bought an airplane ticket, spent two weeks preparing ideas for new songs, packed his bags, and headed east to Nashville. When he arrived, he encountered just one little problem. The songwriter never showed up.

But Blume had the beginning of about a half dozen new songs in his back pocket and he wasn't about to give up now. A publisher friend realized Blume's dilemma, felt bad about it, and arranged for Blume to work with another writer who just happened to be in the office at the time. A. J. Masters was the songwriter's name, and within 45 minutes of their first meeting, the two turned out a song that became a top-five country single. The song was called "Change My Mind" and was performed first by The Oak Ridge Boys and later as a top-five hit for John Barry.

This was the song that led to Blume's success as a song-writer. He landed a job working full-time as a staff writer for a music publishing company. The company has offices all over the world and produces pop, R&B, and country music. The opportunity led to more hits for Blume and great success as a songwriter. By the way, if you ever visit Blume's house, make sure you ring the doorbell. You'll hear a few lines from the song that changed Blume's life: "Change My Mind"!

Some of Blume's other big hits include two songs for Britney Spears—"I'll Never Stop Loving You" and "Dear Diary" (cowritten with Britney herself)—and one for the Backstreet Boys called "Back to Your Heart." After almost 20 years in the business, Blume was an overnight success!

FUTURE SONGWRITERS BEWARE

Blume doesn't pull any punches. When he talks with aspiring songwriters, he is careful to tell it like it really is and likes to share what he's learned throughout the years. Blume says that there are six steps to making it as a songwriter:

1. Use successful song structure.
2. Write lyrics that effectively communicate what's in your heart.
3. Compose memorable melodies.
4. Produce demos that demonstrate the potential of your song.
5. Take care of business.
6. Develop persistence and realistic expectations.

You'll find all the juicy details in Blume's book, *6 Steps to Songwriting Success: Comprehensive Guide to Writing and Marketing Hit Songs* (New York: Billboard Books, 1999). Follow this advice, and maybe you'll see Blume at the top!

For additional information and songwriting tips, visit Blume's website at http://www.jasonblume.com.

Costume Designer

WHAT IS A COSTUME DESIGNER?

A costume designer is part fashion designer, part history professor, part seamstress, part artist, part researcher, and part accountant. A big job? You bet! Costume designers are responsible for either acquiring or creating all the costumes worn in any kind of a production. It could be a ballet, a Broadway musical, a movie, a music video, a television show, or a stage play. Sometimes costumes are made from scratch; other times they are scrounged from flea markets, antique shops, or trendy boutiques.

It all starts with a production and a plan. Once a costume designer is hired to costume a certain type of production, he or she has to learn all about the production. This often involves meeting with the producer or director to find out about the play and what their expectations are. Reading the script helps the designer understand what the show is all about. Issues such as budget will also be ironed out at these early meetings. Once these important discussions are over, the real work begins.

55

First on the designer's drawing board is research. Historically accurate costumes help define a production's place in time and make the story authentic and more believable for an audience. For example, if a production is set in the 1700s, think powdered wigs and corsets. On the other hand, if it's set in 1970, think bell bottoms and leisure suits. Meticulous research often means the difference between mediocre costumes and magnificent ones.

Next up is finding out if the needed costumes are already available to rent or purchase or if new costumes must be created. Contacting suppliers and vendors to secure the necessary costumes at an acceptable price that fits in the budget is one part of this process.

When a production calls for original costumes, the process becomes even more involved. Making sketches for each costume is the first step. Then patterns are cut. Fabrics, dyes, and other materials are selected and purchased. Then it's time to actually construct the costumes and fit them to the performers who will be wearing them. It's often a hectic and exciting process as ideas take form and a visual image of the production emerges.

What is the costume designer's role in all this? It depends on the size of the production. For large, commercial projects with big budgets, the designer may supervise a staff of assistants who do much of the actual hands-on work. The costume designer's role is more that of creative director and chief decision maker. For smaller productions, a costume designer may be responsible for everything.

In any case, meeting tight deadlines, communicating ideas, keeping within a budget, and finding the best sources for costumes or supplies are part of the job. The hours can be long and crazy at times, but the results can be very rewarding. A balance of artistic talent and business sense is common to most good costume designers. On the artistic side, an exhaustive knowledge of fashion design, art, and history is extremely useful. Sketching and sewing come with the territory too. An eye for spotting treasures on frequent shopping expeditions is not only fun but also a great asset for a successful costume designer.

On the business side, excellent interpersonal skills help in working with everyone from directors and suppliers to dancers and seamstresses. Making and sticking to a budget is a must. It also helps to be able to stay cool, calm, and collected under pressure.

Generally, costume designers are very well educated. Many have degrees in fashion, art design, or art history with advanced degrees in theater or theater design. Because costume designers are required to have such a broad base of knowledge, a college degree, while not absolutely required, is highly advisable.

Costume designers often start out as interns or work for little or no pay to get experience. As with all art-related jobs, a good portfolio (a book with photographs of your work) is essential. Costume designers are usually self-employed and work on a project basis, so good contacts and marketing can mean the difference between starving and thriving in this line of work. Since it's not unusual to have lags between projects, some costume designers supplement their income by teaching in college or high school theater departments, writing, or doing research for others.

As hubs of the entertainment industry, Hollywood and New York are probably the best places to find costume design jobs. But there are also opportunities in community theater, college and university theater programs, and in the arts venues of most mid- to large-size cities. Designers are also hired to design costumes for children's dance recitals and theater productions.

TRY IT OUT

SEW WHAT!
What are you going to be for Halloween this year? How about making your own costume (or for one of your siblings)? You'll find lots of ideas on-line at the Costume Site at http://www.milieux.com/costume/costume2.html. If you don't find something that tickles your fancy at this website try, The Costume Page at http://members.aol.com/nebula5. costume.html or the International Costumer's Guide at http://www.costume.org.

Books are another source of inspiration and instruction. Here are a few to try:

Dearing, Shirley. *Elegantly Frugal Costumes: The Poor Man's Do-It-Yourself Costume Maker's Guide.* Colorado Springs, Colo.: Meriwether Publishing, 1992.

Govier, Jacquie, and Gill Davies. *Create Your Own Stage Costumes.* Westport, Conn.: Heinemann, 1996.

Litherland, Janet, and Sue McAnally. *Broadway Costumes on a Budget: Big-Time Ideas for Amateur Producers.* Colorado Springs, Colo.: Meriwether Publishing, 1996.

Rogers, Bard. *Costuming Made Easy: How to Make Theatrical Costumes from Cast-off Clothing.* Colorado Springs, Colo.: Meriwether Publishing, 1999.

If you are too old (or too cool) for Halloween costumes, think about inviting a few friends over for a costume party and use these resources to come up with an awesome getup.

THE SHOW MUST GO ON
Volunteer to help with costumes for your school's next production. Get as involved as the person in charge will let you. Hint: An overworked teacher will never turn down good help. Also many places of worship do musical performances for the holidays. Check these places as well as your local theater groups to see if you can help with costumes.

TIME TRAVEL
Camp out at your computer when you've got plenty of time and immerse yourself in the abundant costume resources on the Internet. Start at the Costume Gallery's Research Library at http://www.costumegallery.com/research.htm. They have on-line articles on fashion dating back to 1580, costume portfolios on everything from the *Titanic* to the 1970s and research organized by time and topic.

The Costume Institute of the Metropolitan Museum of Art site at http://www.metmuseum.org/collections/department.asp?dep=8 has photographs and descriptions of costumes from different historical periods.

Edith Head costumed some of Hollywood's biggest stars. Visit http://www.edithhead.com to learn about her and see some of her work.

The Men with Big Hair site at http://www.costumes.org/subwebs/mwbh will lead you to a listing of interesting sites related to costumes and the movies.

For a website loaded with designs, costume history, how-to advice, and links to many other costume sites, visit www.costumes.org.

CLASSROOM COSTUMES
Imagine that you've been hired to create the costumes for a typical all-American middle school classroom. The producer

wants you to put your ideas together in a notebook to present at an important meeting with the all-star cast. Find pictures in magazines, catalogs, and the websites of some your favorite shops and put them in your notebook. Be sure to include descriptions and ideas that reflect all the different styles you'd find in a group of young teens—from preppy to geeky.

A FASHION FIELD DAY

There are tons of books about fashion and costumes. Use them to start developing your costuming know-how. Begin with some of the titles listed below.

Baker, Georgia O'Daniel, and Helen Redel Pullen. *A Handbook of Costume Drawing: A Guide to Drawing the Period Figure for Costume Design Students.* Woburn, Mass.: Focal Press, 1992.

Harrison, Mary Kent. *How to Dress Dancers: Costume Techniques for Dance.* Hightstown, N.J.: Princeton Book Company, 1999.

Ingham, Rosemary, and Elizabeth Covey. *The Costume Designer's Handbook: A Complete Guide for Amateur and Professional Costume Designers.* New York: Quite Specific Media Group, 1992.

Jackson, Sheila. *Costumes for the Stage: A Complete Handbook for Every Kind of Play.* San Francisco: New Amsterdam Books, 1990.

Leese, Elizabeth. *Costume Design in the Movies: An Illustrated Guide to the Work of 157 Great Designers.* Mineola, N.Y.: Dover Publications, 1991.

Pecktal, Lynn, and Tony Walton. *Costume Design: Techniques of Modern Masters.* New York: Back Stage Books, 1999.

You'll find more ideas about careers with clothes in this book:

Maura, Lucia. *Careers for Fashion Plates & Other Trendsetters.* Lincolnwood, Ill.: VGM Horizons, 1996.

CHECK IT OUT

Association of Performing Arts and Craftspeople
661 Tenth Avenue, Suite 4D
New York, New York 10036
http://www.theaterweb/ATAC

Costume Society of America
55 Edgewater Drive
P.O. Box 73
Earleville, Maryland 21919
(800) CSA-9447
http://www.costumesocietyamerica.com

International Costumers Guild, Inc.
7348 Milwood Avenue, Suite 1
Canoga Park, California 91303-3426
http://www.costume.org/

Performing Arts Resources
88 East Third Street, Suite 19
New York, New York 10003
http://www.members.aol.com/perfrtrsrc

GET ACQUAINTED

Ronda Grim,
Costume Designer

CAREER PATH

CHILDHOOD ASPIRATION: To do something in fashion.

FIRST JOB: Worked at her family's retail business.

CURRENT JOB: Costume designer and owner of Dragonfly Design Studio.

CHANGING HATS

Ronda Grim wears a lot of different hats as costume designer and owner of Dragonfly Design Studio, an on-line costume shop. Her day usually starts at about 9:00 A.M. She spends part of the morning reading e-mail, downloading orders customers have placed on her website, and running credit cards. Then she fills orders with premade costumes she has in stock, boxes them up, and prepares them for shipping. Next she schedules time to make custom orders. Around lunchtime she makes a run to the UPS to ship out packages. Afternoons are usually spent creating custom costumes.

Grim's customers are pretty diverse. She has created costumes for theater groups, ballet troupes, renaissance fairs, Middle Ages recreation groups, and sci-fi conventions. One of the jobs she is most proud of is creating 40 original Celtic masks for a dance company.

ALL DRESSED UP WITH SOMEWHERE TO GO

Grim loved playing dress-up as a child and always knew that she wanted to do something in fashion. She spent a year in college in the theater department before moving to Georgia so her husband could work on his master's degree. Needing to help put him through college, Grim worked retail at first and did some design work on the side. Her husband worked in the scene shop at one of the university theaters, so when a position for assistant costume designer became available, Grim applied and got the job.

After her husband graduated, they moved to Oregon, and Grim took a job at a fabric store—mostly to get a discount on fabrics—and started building a freelance costume design business. When the theater department at a nearby college lost their costume designer, Grim took over and ran the costume shop for three years.

She continued to work freelance for other theater groups, churches, and a number of organizations. Eventually that business evolved into Dragonfly Design Studio, the web-based costume shop she runs today.

A WORLD OF HER OWN

Grim likes working in a "fantasy world." As a costume design-er, she finds there is always something new to be done. She loves the creative challenge of the work and takes special pleasure in figuring out how to do something that "can't" be done.

On the down side, being self-employed often means work-ing long hours. It can also be tough to be creative on demand when trying to meet tight deadlines. Looking back, she wishes there had been some sort of guidebook on how to run a costume design business when she was starting out. It would have been saved a lot of time and mistakes early on if she had known some of the business basics such as dealing with credit cards and pricing costumes.

PLAN B

Grim's advice for those pursuing a career in costume design is to go to college. This is a good idea for two reasons. First, it can help you refine skills and learn more about theater arts and costuming. Second, Grim thinks that a degree gives you more options when you are ready to move on to something new in your career.

Dance Instructor

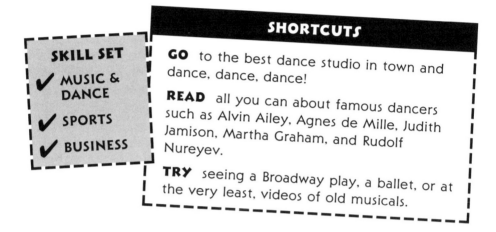

SKILL SET

✔ MUSIC & DANCE

✔ SPORTS

✔ BUSINESS

GO to the best dance studio in town and dance, dance, dance!

READ all you can about famous dancers such as Alvin Ailey, Agnes de Mille, Judith Jamison, Martha Graham, and Rudolf Nureyev.

TRY seeing a Broadway play, a ballet, or at the very least, videos of old musicals.

WHAT IS A DANCE INSTRUCTOR?

Dance is sometimes a sport, and sometimes it's an art form. Sometimes dance is a means of religious expression, and sometimes it's a type of cultural identity. But it's always lots of fun. Dance instructors are the people who link dance in all its forms and expressions from one generation to the next.

Dance instructors are part dancer, part teacher, part coach, and sometimes even part businessperson or administrator. As dancers, their job is to introduce students to the techniques and skills necessary to perform a particular type of dance such as ballet, jazz, folk, ethnic, or modern. As teachers, their job is to share the history and traditions associated with various types of dance. As coaches, they constantly try to instill a sense of self-discipline and self-esteem in each of their students. And as businesspeople or administrators, they may be responsible for running a dance studio, organizing performances, and planning programs.

Many dance instructors dance professionally before they start teaching. In fact, all dance instructors should be more than proficient as dancers themselves. Dance is not a subject you can muddle your way through by reading a book the night before class. Showing is as important as knowing when it comes to introducing intricate dance steps to students at all levels.

Student ability levels, by the way, are another thing that distinguish one dance instructor from another. Some dance instructors work primarily with beginning students—whether children or adults—while others may work with more advanced students or a combination of both. Very experienced instructors may choose to work with professional dancers or dance troupes. They may also help serious dancers train to become professional dancers.

Dance instructors work in a variety of places including public schools, professional dance companies, studios, other arts-related organizations, and colleges. Some dance instructors set up studios in their homes where they work with individuals or small groups of students.

Those who teach in public schools generally must complete a college program and obtain a teaching certificate in order to qualify. Various types of college programs provide good training for a dance teacher: dance, fine arts, dance composition, and theater arts. In settings other than a public school, the only requirements are personal training, experience, and a love of dance—which may not be as easy as it sounds.

Of course, it doesn't hurt to have the patience of an angel, the discipline of a drill sergeant, and the diplomacy of a politician as well. Teaching dance is very much a people business. Whether working with talented aspiring dancers, who would rather be dancing than anything else in the world, or working with klutzes, who are dancing only because their parents make them, dance instructors must be able to bring out the best in each student.

TRY IT OUT

VIRTUAL FIELD TRIP

So you don't live anywhere near Saratoga Springs, New York, home to the National Museum of Dance? Don't let that stop you from taking a field trip to the only museum in America devoted exclusively to dance. Ballet, Broadway, modern, jazz, ethnic, and tap—they are all to be found on-line at http://www.dancemuseum.org. Browse all you want and see if you can successfully complete the worksheet found when you click the "worksheet" icon.

ON-LINE TANGO

Looking for a few good websites about dance? You might as well start at the CyberDance website. With a collection of more than 3,500 links to classical ballet and modern dance resources, this is a great place to start. Find it at http://www. cyberdance.org.

Warm up with all those links and two-step over to some of these websites as well:

- Dance Links at http://www.dancer.com/dance-links
- Dance Online at http://danceonline.com
- Dance Net at http://www.dance.net
- Dance Vision at http://www.dancevision.com

For a look at some on-line dance magazines boogie over to some of these sites:

- Dance Spirit at http://www.dancespirit.com
- Dance Teacher Magazine at http://www. dance-teacher.com
- Pointe Magazine Online at http://www. pointemagazine.com
- InMotion magazine at http://www.inmotionline.com

A DANCER'S FIRST STEPS

Did you know that nearly every position in ballet begins or ends with one of five patterns? You can't be a dancer until you know these positions. Learn them if you don't know them already, and then teach them to someone else.

Besides the obvious choice of learning these steps at a dance studio, you can also try the do-it-yourself method by carefully following instructions included in books such as these:

Bussell, Darcy, and Patricia Linton. *The Young Dancer.* New York: DK Publishing, 1994.

Grant, Gail. *Technical Manual and Dictionary of Classical Ballet.* Mineola, N.Y.: Dover Publications, 1982.

MacKie, Joyce. *Basic Ballet.* New York: Penguin USA, 1980.

Sibley, Antoinette. *Step-by-Step Ballet Class: The Official Illustrated Guide.* Lincolnwood, Ill.: NTC Publishing, 1994.

Or go on-line to the National Ballet School's dancer's first steps page at http://www.nationalballetschool.org/pages/firststeps/index.html.

Once you've got the basics down pat, try making up a dance routine for one of your favorite songs and teaching it to a group of friends. Feel free to use some of these basic dance steps but be sure to add lots of your own ideas as well.

DANCE AT FIRST SIGHT

Dance at its best is beautiful to experience—both as a participant and as an observer. While learning to be a participant in dance is certainly key to success as a dance teacher, so is learning how to observe it. It's those precise, carefully choreographed movements of a well-trained dancer that spark the magic in any dance. Dance teachers must develop a practiced eye to notice all these subtle nuances and encourage them in their dancers.

Start now to develop keen observation skills with some of the following activities. First, take advantage of every opportunity to observe dance. Watch young children at your dance studio and see how they learn new steps. Watch professional dancers in plays, movies, arts festivals, and the like. Go to art museums and see how artists portray dancers. Look at dance as if it were a wonderful story being told on stage and see if you can "read between the lines" to understand it better.

Second, become a student of movement, which, after all, is the essence of dance. Sit at the mall and watch people as they wander by. Notice how you "read" various emotions from the way people move and walk. Look at how the lines of their bodies change as they sit or bend or juggle heavy packages.

Third, enjoy good photographs of dancers in motion in books such as these:

———————————

Balanchine, George, and Francis Mason. *101 Stories of the Great Ballets.* New York: Doubleday, 1975.

Coffey, Judith. *Ballet, Tap, and All That Jazz!: The Essential Guide for Today's Young Dancer, Cheerleader, Skater, and Gymnast.* Jonesboro, Ark.: Rainbow Educational Concepts, 1998.

Feldman, Jane. *I Am a Dancer.* New York: Random House, 1999.

Jessel, Camilla. *Ballet School.* New York: Viking Children's Books, 2000.

Lee, Sandy. *At the Ballet: On Stage, Backstage.* New York: Universe Publishing, 1998.

———————————

WILL WORK FOR DANCE

If you're thinking about a career as a dance instructor, you may not have to wait until you grow up to find out if you like it. Chances are that the instructors where you take dance lessons would be willing to allow you to assist them in classes for younger or less experienced children if you would just let them know you're interested. You may also find opportunities to help stage school plays and productions at a preschool or child center. You'll never know until you ask.

Gain some experience and you might eventually be able to dance yourself into a part-time job as an assistant at a studio or a tutor to other young dancers.

THE WORD ON DANCE

Like other types of professions, dance has its own lingo. Dancers soon learn that there's a big difference between adagio and allegro. Learn to speak dance with the American Ballet Theater's on-line dancer's dictionary at http://www.abt.org/dictionary/terms.html. Use it to find out what the following terms mean:

- ☼ Arabesque
- ☼ Barre
- ☼ Fondu
- ☼ Pirouette
- ☼ Plié
- ☼ Relevé

CHECK IT OUT

American Dance Guild
P.O. Box 2006
Lenox Hill Station
New York, New York 10021
http://www.americandanceguild.org

Dance Educators of America
P.O. Box 607
Pelham, New York 10803
http://www.deadance.com

Dance Theater Workshop
219 West 19th Street
New York, New York 10011
http://www.danceforce.org

Dance USA
1156 15th Street NW, Suite 820
Washington, D.C. 20005
http://www.danceusa.org

National Dance Association
1900 Association Drive
Reston, Virginia 22091
http://www.aahperd.org/nda/nda-main.html

Professional Dance Teachers Association
P.O. Box 38
Waldwick, New Jersey 07463
http://www.pdta.org

GET ACQUAINTED

Kirstie Tice, Dance Instructor

CAREER PATH

CHILDHOOD ASPIRATION: To be a performer.

FIRST JOB: Dormouse in a community theater production of *Cinderella*.

CURRENT JOB: Artistic director, Broadway Dance Project.

OFF TO AN EARLY START

Dancing came naturally to Kirstie Tice. Moving around is something that has always made her happy. She had a love of movement and a tendency to ham it up whenever she got the chance.

Also Tice's mom worked for a talent agency and had the inside track on all kinds of local performance opportunities, so it's no wonder that Tice started acting in commercials at the ripe old age of seven. That first professional acting job was for a commercial featuring Popeye's fried chicken. Tice's role? To lick her lips and act like she'd just eaten the best fried chicken she'd ever tasted!

Before her career in commercials was over, Tice had performed in 30 regional commercials and five national ones— including commercials for big names such as Burger King, Coca-Cola, Dr Pepper, and Panasonic.

Commercials weren't the only stage that young Tice used to share her budding talent. She also performed in community theater productions and professional dinner theaters. Tice says that all that early experience was like getting paid to learn how to act.

Tice credits her mom for being the instigator of all these early opportunities. But she's quick to point out that her mother was never a stage mother. She facilitated opportunities when Tice wanted to pursue them. She provided rides, information, tips on diction and speaking, and let Tice call the shots about what she wanted to do. She was even supportive of Tice's decision to take two years off from dance classes when at the age of 10 she was burned out and wanted a break from being a "bunhead."

HONING HER CRAFT

When it came time to go to college, Tice was accepted into three schools with exceptional dance programs. One was in New York, one was in California, and one was in North Carolina. She choose to attend the one in North Carolina because it wasn't located in a major metropolitan city, and Tice felt that she could focus more on her studies without the lure of a big city distracting her.

Tice's last year of college was spent doing an apprenticeship with a dance troupe's European tour of *West Side Story*.

Tice was one of five dancers selected out of 500 who auditioned for the coveted spot. When she arrived for her first rehearsal, she was initially terrified to discover that she'd assigned to be the "swing." The "swing" has to learn every single role in the production and be ready to fill in whenever any other dancer is unable to perform. In this case, Tice had to learn all the dances for eight roles!

After spending several years touring Europe, Tice won the role of the white cat in the Broadway production of *Cats*. It was a demanding role that required complete concentration—in eight shows a week performed in theaters across America.

She later went back to Europe as dance captain for the *West Side Story* group. All in all, Tice spent eight years on the road. The gypsy years, Tice calls them, because during that time she never had an apartment of her own, no pillow, no telephone, and no car. She says she lived out of a suitcase, but don't feel sorry for her. She also got to see the world and do what she loved best—dance!

A PLACE TO CALL HOME

Eight years was enough for Tice. At that point, she decided it was time to settle down and pursue new challenges as a dancer. That's where the dance instructor part comes into the story.

After completing a rigorous teacher training program at the National Dance Institute (a phenomenal program that Tice heartily recommends—you can find information at http://www.nationaldance.org) and with some help from friends, Tice started her own dance studio.

Never mind that she'd never taught a class in her life! Tice just knew that she wanted to provide opportunities for people to enjoy life and to create a dance program where not one person went unnoticed. She committed herself to putting 100 percent of her energy into her classes 100 percent of the time. Then she opened her doors . . . and nobody came.

Well, almost nobody. Sometimes the classes had a couple of people in them. Tice says she cried every day for the first year she was in business. She was sure that nobody "loved her," and that she'd never make it as a dance instructor.

But she continued to give it all she had, and word got around. By the next year, classes were filling up, and by the year after that, there was a waiting list for many of Tice's classes. Now she has several other dance instructors working for her, and her studio has a reputation for being the best studio in town.

Teaching isn't the only way that dance fills Tice's life. She also choreographs productions for a variety of local theaters and colleges. And she continues her role as assistant director for the *West Side Story* troupe.

TICE'S TIDBITS OF ADVICE

Tice has a couple of suggestions for aspiring dancers and dance instructors. First, she insists that every dancer see performances of *Cats* and *A Chorus Line*, two all-time Broadway favorites. Second, she suggests that you take time to study the classics in ballet, art, and literature where she says you are sure to find inspiration as a dancer. And finally, she encourages you to get involved in school or community theater productions—but not just as a dancer. Tice thinks it's a great idea to get as much experience onstage, backstage, behind-the-scenes—anywhere you can learn all you can about performing and what it takes to put on a production. That way you'll be prepared for anything when the bright lights beckon!

Dancer

SKILL SET

✔ **MUSIC & DANCE**

✔ **SPORTS**

✔ **TALKING**

GO on-line and to the library to find out all you can about famous dancers such as Martha Graham, Alvin Ailey, and Rudolf Nureyev

READ *Dance* magazine. For an on-line version, visit http://www.dancemagazine.com.

TRY learning a new dance step such as salsa, jive, or swing. Sign up for classes at your local recreation center or dance studio. And go on-line for tips at http://www. bustamove.com.

WHAT IS A DANCER?

Dance is one of humankind's earliest forms of communication. It's been used in virtually every civilization to express ideas, stories, and to celebrate life. Professional dancers are talented people who make a living in this age-old but always new form of communication.

Dancers do their thing in a variety of settings including musical productions, operas, television shows, movies, music videos, and commercials. Dancers take the stage onboard cruise ships, at dinner theaters, in entertainment theme parks, and in resorts. Some conduct special performances at festivals and schools while others travel the world in Broadway productions. As is the case for other types of performing arts, the larger the city, the more opportunities you're likely to find. New York, Los Angeles, Las Vegas, and Chicago are particularly big dance meccas. However, many small and midsize cities have thriving cultural arts programs where dancers find plenty of work.

Dancing tends to be a career for the young—or at least the young at heart. It's hard, physically demanding work. Dancers often stop performing by their late thirties but may stay in the profession by assuming roles as choreographers, dance teachers, coaches, or artistic directors. Of course, there are exceptions to every rule. Many dancers are still hoofing it well into their fifties and beyond.

Unlike other careers in which serious training doesn't usually begin until after high school or in college, dance training often begins as early as five years old. Ballet requires more intensive training than other forms of dance, but most dancers are fairly serious about dance by their mid-teens.

Many, but not all, dancers continue their education and training at a college or university that offers degrees in subjects such as music, dance, theater, or fine arts. There are pros and cons to spending prime dancing years in school. Some dancers find that getting a degree makes the transition into another career easier once their dancing career starts to ebb. Others find that they want to dance while they can and hold off on college training. This is a decision that requires plenty of thought. Those thinking about a career in dance should

seek counsel from trusted advisers such as parents, dance instructors, and mentors.

Whichever educational path a dancer may choose, he or she must get as much training as possible. Healthy lifestyles that nurture and nourish the body and mind help ensure longer, more productive careers. Some dancers find that dance is much more than a way to earn a living; it is quite often a way of life.

TRY IT OUT

STORIES BEHIND THE SONGS

Dance is often used to tell a story. Many intriguing tales are spun in operas. Opera, by the way, is something an aspiring dancer will want to know about. Here are some resources to make the learning process easy:

Plotkin, Fred. *Opera 101: A Complete Guide to Learning and Loving Opera.* New York: Hyperion, 1994.

Pogue, David, and Scott Speck. *Opera for Dummies.* New York: IDG Books Worldwide, 1997.

Simon, Henry W. *100 Great Operas and Their Stories.* New York: Doubleday, 1989.

You might also do well to investigate the works of William Shakespeare. The *Shakespeare Can Be Fun* series is a great place to start. There are titles for *A Midsummer Night's Dream, Macbeth, Romeo and Juliet, Twelfth Night,* and *The Tempest.* The series is written by Lois Burdett and published by Firefly Books.

You may also want to look with new interest at the classics you are assigned to read in literature classes. Think about how each story might be told through dance.

Pick one of these stories or one from a book you've read recently, and make up a dance that tells at least part of what the story is all about. A Harry Potter waltz, anyone?

VIRTUAL DANCE

Find out what it's like to train with some of the best dance companies in the country at some of these websites:

- School of American Ballet at http://www.sabl.org
- Alvin Ailey American Dance Theater at http://www.alvinailey.org
- The Joffrey Ballet School at http://www.joffreyballet.com
- Martha Graham School of Contemporary Dance at http://www.marthagrahamcenter.org

These and other dance schools offer a wonderful assortment of dance training programs. One way to get a tiny taste of what's it like to be a professional dancer is to enroll in a summer dance intensive. These programs tend to run for at least two weeks at a time and each day is full of dance classes. Ask if your local studio or community arts center will offer such a program. And go on-line to find out about all kinds of summer dance "camp" options at http://www.dancecollective.com or at Peterson's Summer Opportunities for Kids and Teenagers website at http://www.petersons.com/summerop/ssector.html.

THE HARD QUESTIONS

A career in dancing isn't for everyone, even those who are fantastic dancers. You'll want to take a good hard look at what it takes to be a professional dancer before you make the decision. Some resources that can help include:

Boling, Bobby. *A Dancer's Manual: A Motivational Guide to Professional Dancing.* Studio City, Calif.: Rafter Publications, 2000.

Hamilton, Linda. *Advice for Dancers: Emotional Counsel and Practical Strategies.* New York: Jossey-Bass, Inc., 1998.

Mirault, Dan. *Dancing for a Living Two: Where the Jobs Are, What They Pay, What Choreographers Want, What to Ask.* Studio City, Calif.: Rafter Publications, 1999.

An especially helpful on-line resource is Grover Dale's answers4dancers website, which, as its name suggests, provides answers and resources to common questions asked by young, hopeful dancers. This website can be found at http://www.answers4dancers.com. Another website you'll want to visit is called The Career Resource for Dancers at http://www.dancecollective.com

CHECK IT OUT

American Dance Guild
P.O. Box 2006
Lenox Hill Station
New York, New York 10021
http://www.americandanceguild.org

American Dance Legacy Foundation
P.O. Box 1897
Providence, Rhode Island 02912
http://www.brown.edu/Departments/Theatre_Speech_Dance/
Amer._Dance_Legacy_Inst.html

Dance USA
1156 15th Street NW, Suite 820
Washington, D.C. 20005
http://www.danceusa.org

National Dance Association
1900 Association Drive
Reston, Virginia 22091
http://www.aahperd.org/nda/nda-main.html

National Dance Council of America
824 St. Marks Avenue
Westfield, New Jersey 07090
http://www.ndca.org

GET ACQUAINTED

LeVon Campbell, Dancer

CAREER PATH

CHILDHOOD ASPIRATION: To be a teacher.

FIRST JOB: Dancing the part of Stromboli (Pinocchio's nemesis) in a Disney on Parade™ production.

CURRENT JOB: Associate artistic director, Dallas Black Dance Theatre.

A FATEFUL FLUKE

LeVon Campbell never expected to become a dancer. He grew up in northeast Chicago's rough-and-tumble world. Most people assume that kids from the projects don't do ballet.

But fate had a different idea. Campbell started dancing in 1967 and he hasn't stopped since. It started innocently enough when Campbell and a bunch of his friends starting goofing around at his house. He'd play the piano, and everyone would dance and just have a good time.

About the same time this makeshift dance troupe noticed that they were pretty good, their high school announced auditions for the annual international jamboree. The group auditioned, made the cut, and shared the stage on the big night with other talented performers from their diverse school community. No big deal. It was just for fun.

What Campbell didn't realize at the time was that the audience included two people who would soon change his life forever. Katherine Dunham, one of the world's most respected dancers, choreographers, and teachers, was one. Sidney

Harris, father of one of Campbell's classmates and writer for the *Chicago Tribune* was another.

The next day Campbell received a phone call from Mr. Harris. Mr. Harris wanted to know if Campbell would mind being recommended as a recipient for a Percy scholarship (this scholarship was established by Senator Charles Percy in memory of his daughter Virgina, a dancer who was murdered). The scholarship review committee was comprised of members of some of the most wealthy and powerful families in America—Kennedys, Rockefellers, and Vanderbilts. At the time, the scholarship awarded funds to cover costs associated with helping dance students attain professional goals. Class, clothes, rent, medical bills—everything was covered so that the student could fully devote himself or herself to learning their craft.

Did Campbell want to be considered for such an honor? Sure. Who wouldn't? But Campbell never really expected the phone call that eventually came. "Congratulations. You've been selected . . ."

FULL STEAM AHEAD

That's when the boy from the projects started taking ballet. Remember Katherine Dunham, the famous dancer sitting in the audience during Campbell's dance debut at the school jamboree? She became one of Campbell's first dance instructors.

Campbell's life may well have turned out quite differently if it hadn't been for the gifts of benefactors who really believed in him. However, all their generosity couldn't change one simple fact: Campbell was still a kid from the projects. At first, the other kids in the neighborhood gave him a lot of grief about dancing. He remembers being chased home from dance classes a few times. But one day he stopped running. He told his tormentors, "Look, this is who I am. This is what I've got to do and you're gonna have to get used to it." Get used to it they did, and Campbell was on his way to a lifetime of dance.

Campbell's training started in Chicago, where he studied with some of the best. Still a teenager, he also got to spend summers training in New York. In 1970, he left for what was supposed to be a short visit to New York. But he says he knew as soon as crossed the George Washington Bridge that he'd never go back.

NEW YORK, HERE I COME

New York brought more opportunities to dance. First was an opportunity to dance with the Disney on Parade production. Campbell danced his way throughout Mexico and the United States as bad guy Stromboli.

Those early years also brought Campbell the chance to dance and study with the world renowned Alvin Ailey American Dance Theater.

DECADES OF DANCE

Through the years, Campbell's incredible career has included dancing in Broadway shows, touring with legends such as Lena Horne and Eartha Kitt, and a long and enjoyable stint with *Sesame Street Live.* He started out dancing as Cookie Monster but eventually took over as performance director and traveled with the company for more than 10 years.

One of Campbell's most recent roles was that of Porgy in Gershwin's *Porgy and Bess* with the Dallas Black Dance Theatre. That role led to his current job as associate artistic director for the company.

IN A WORD

Campbell boils down his success as a dancer to one word: focus. Even as a teen, Campbell had a single-minded, whole-hearted focus on his goal to become a dancer. He thinks such as focus can help anyone with high hopes for their future. He tells young people: "There's nothing you can't obtain once you set your mind on what you want to do. You alone are responsible for your failures and successes."

For more information about Campbell and the Dallas Black Dance Theatre visit http://www.dbdt.com.

Disc Jockey

WHAT IS A DISC JOCKEY?

They wake us up in the morning. They talk to us on the way to school. They keep us company at night. They entertain us at dances and weddings. Who are they? Disc jockeys (DJs), of course!

Disc jockeys or announcers are the people behind the voices you hear on the radio, in television announcements, and in nightclubs or big party-type events. Whether reading a news bulletin, introducing a commercial, interviewing a celebrity, or cracking a joke, DJs have to stay on their toes. Dead air time is not a good thing. DJs keep things rolling for hours at time—informing and entertaining their listeners.

It's almost like putting a giant time puzzle together every day with each of the pieces representing the right mix of songs, gab, and news. Everything must be timed down to the second so that one segment flows into the next. Keeping things flowing smoothly requires careful planning. Everything from the songs to be played, the commercials to be run, and the topics to be discussed are planned before hand. DJs often use a script or cue sheet to keep themselves on track.

What does it takes to be a DJ? Three things mostly—personality plus, a great speaking voice, and a love of music. With those bases covered, there are several ways to get ready for a career in radio. Some DJs just do it. They start out working the school dances, emceeing school events, or announcing at sports games; discover a knack for this type of work; and move on to a small local radio station or DJ business of their own. A little luck and lots of hard work, they build a career from the ground up through on-the-job experience.

Other DJs choose to get formal training at a college or in a vocational training program where the focus is on broadcasting or communications. These types of programs offer opportunities to refine skills, learn the technical aspects of the work, and get some experience.

There are also a number of broadcasting schools that train DJs and other types of broadcast technicians in a relatively short amount of time. These may or may not be a good option. Some offer solid, legitimate programs, others are fly-by-night scams that are best avoided. Be sure to check out the reputation of any type of training program with your state's attorney general's office or the Better Business Bureau.

Regardless of the training, disc jockeys must obtain a license from the Federal Communications Commission (FCC) in order to go on air. This is pretty much just a formality involving submitting a letter and application and does not require a test.

Celebrity status is often one of the perks of this profession. DJs often garner a certain amount of fame, at least in the communities where they work. Making personal appearances at community events, parades, sports events, fund-raisers, and store openings are part of building an audience and keeping them happy.

Moving up the career ladder, some DJs become radio talk show hosts. Whether it's morning chitchat, hard-driving political commentary, or celebrity interviews the show is theirs to fill and build. It's considered quite a coup to reach this level of popularity.

TRY IT OUT

THE RIGHT MIX

Do you have what it takes to be a radio DJ? Take this fun online test and find out: http://www.radiodiscjockey.com. According to these "experts," the most important quality for a successful disc jockey is that he or she loves the work.

DJ DEMO

For some realistic practice at what it's like to be a DJ, grab a tape recorder and a blank tape, find a quiet place, and try some of these on-air exercises:

- Pick a favorite song and think of an interesting way to introduce it to radio listeners. Mention an interesting tidbit about the performer, make up a mushy dedication to someone, or whatever you can think of that would encourage listeners to stay tuned.
- Make up a short broadcast to complete the sentence "Today's late breaking news is . . ." Record yourself

announcing good news and bad news. How are your voice, your delivery, and your choice of words affected by the type of news you are conveying?

☼ For a real challenge, turn off the sound during a television broadcast of a sports event or music awards show and take over as the announcer. Give a play-by-play account of all the action. It's not as easy as it looks!

TALKING BOOKS

There's more than one way to read a book. Those who are blind, have trouble reading, or other learning problems often enjoy curling up with a good book—on tape. Talk to your teacher or the school librarian to find out if you can help someone out by reading some of their assignments to them on tape. This activity can help others while it helps you train to be a DJ. Use a clear, strong voice and make what you are reading more interesting by changing your tone and using different voices for various characters.

RADIO ROUNDUP

Here's the plan. First, tune in to your area's all-talk radio station. Most areas have at least one. For on-line lists of resources visit Talk: An Internet Radio List Station Guide at http://www.internetradiolist.com/rg/talk; the Radio Resources on the Internet website at http://www.lib.ua.edu/smr/radio 1.htm; or Radio Stations on the Web at http://www.freedom. simplenet.com/stationfinders.htm.

Next, get a little notebook to keep tabs on what you find out as you tune in to several different types of talk shows. Listen to an early morning chat show, a sports broadcast, a straight news broadcast, a call-in issue-oriented show, and any other interesting formats you can find. As you listen, take note of the station's call letters, the time of the broadcast, the broadcaster's name, and a description of what you think about the show. What are the most interesting features? What would you do differently if you were the announcer? Which type of format seems the most comfortable fit for you?

DJ UNIVERSITY

DJ University is a website that offers several free on-line classes, lectures, and forums to learn how to be a disc jockey. The website address is http://dju.prodj.com. You'll find some interesting resources here and you can't beat the price!

Another cool site full of free tips and advice is the on-line school of radio broadcasting found at http://www.teusplanet.net/public/bytemee/start.htm.

For some radio fun and games be sure to check out the Kids Internet Radio Links at http://www.kir.org/radio.htm.

TUNE IN TO MORE CAREER IDEAS

For more ideas about various on air and behind the scenes in radio look for these books in your local library:

Ellis, Elmo. *Opportunities in Broadcasting Careers.* Lincolnwood, Ill.: VGM Career Horizons, 1998.

Morgan, Bradley, J., and Joseph M. Palmisano. *Radio and Television Career Directory: A Practical, One-Step Guide to Getting a Job in Radio and Television.* New York: Gale Research, 1993.

CHECK IT OUT

American Disc Jockey Association
10882 Demar Road
White Plains, Maryland 20695
http://www.adja.org

American Federation of Television and Radio Artists
260 Madison Avenue
New York, New York 10016
http://www.aftra.org

National Academy of Recording Arts and Sciences
3402 Pico Boulevard
Santa Monica, California 90405
http://www.grammy.com

National Association of Broadcast Employees and Technicians
501 Third Street NW
Washington, D.C. 20001
http://www.nabetcwa.org

National Association of Broadcasters
1771 N Street NW
Washington, D.C. 20036
http://www.nab.org

Society of Broadcast Engineers
8445 Keystone Crossing, Suite 140
Indianapolis, Indiana 46248
http://www.sbe.org

GET ACQUAINTED

Lydia Smith, Disc Jockey

CAREER PATH

CHILDHOOD ASPIRATION: To be a performer.

FIRST JOB: Waitress at a neighborhood restaurant.

CURRENT JOB: Program director for ivillage music network.

AN EARLY START

Lydia Smith was born to entertain. The daughter of a Methodist minister and an elementary school teacher, Smith never passed up a chance to shine in the limelight. She got her big chance at the age of five when children at her father's church were asked to take turns singing their favorite

Sunday school songs for the congregation. Smith brought down the house when she jumped on a table and belted out a rousing rendition of "Love Potion #9"!

Classical singing lessons started at age 11 followed by plenty of involvement in school drama and theater productions. When the time came to go to college, Smith started out with a pre-law major. With visions of dazzling courtroom performances dancing in her head, Smith thought that law would be a good way to blend her interest in politics with her flair for the dramatic. It soon became apparent that there was a big difference between TV lawyers and real lawyers, and Smith decided that law wasn't a good fit for her after all.

She finished her college training with degrees (and honors) in religion and humanities. Smith credits her broad liberal arts education to giving her the background she needed to succeed in all kinds of things.

A LITTLE OF THIS, A LITTLE OF THAT

This was lucky because all kinds of things is exactly what Smith did once she graduated from college. At one point she was acting, doing voice-overs for radio commercials, delivering singing telegrams, and working as a costume designer. It was a lot to juggle, but it was fun—and it paid the bills.

Later Smith spent 10 years working in traditional radio broadcasting. That experience led to an opportunity to teach broadcasting at a major university. The teaching led Smith to an awareness of the Internet. She saw it as a new frontier for journalism in general and radio broadcasting in particular.

At about the same time, Smith was affected by another big trend in broadcasting—corporate buyouts. Smith says that three mega-media conglomorates now own about 95 percent of the radio stations in America. When Smith's station was bought, she was out of a job.

All of a sudden she found herself with some extra time on her hands, so Smith enrolled in a web design class. Things fell together from there. As some of the most interesting careers tend to go, one thing led to another. Smith was soon recruited by ivillage.com, an on-line community for women where

her newfound Internet expertise was immediately put to work.

Now Smith hosts a live, on-line radio show for five hours a day, five days a week. She's also program director of the ivillage music network and is responsible (with some much needed help from an assistant) for planning the format and music for the on-line radio station each day.

Smith's show includes a mix of music, requests (e-mailed from all over the world), and in-depth interviews and discussions about issues of importance to women. It's a big job and one that Smith must do well—given that they call her Goddess Lydia.

TUNE IN

Smith's show is aired from 12:00 P.M. to 5:00 P.M. (eastern standard time) during the week. You can tune in on-line at http://www.ivillage.com/ivmn. Go ahead and request a favorite song. Smith says she'd love to hear from you.

And, by the way, if you have hopes of a career like Smith's, here are a few tips from the "goddess" herself.

1. Use your voice. Take voice lessons, speech classes, sing, read poetry out loud—in short, do anything you can to develop an interesting voice. It is, of course, the primarily tool of this trade.
2. Work on yourself. Get to know who you are, what you believe, and what you want out of life. Smith says it's a surefire way to avoid sounding fake on air.
3. Be nice. It will come back to you in good ways. Smith guarantees it!

Grip, Gaffer, and Lighting Technician

SHORTCUTS

GO attend a concert and take special notice of how the lighting affects the mood of the show.

READ the credits at the end of movies. You will see that grips, gaffers and lighting technicians are real people just like you.

TRY taking a photography course to learn how lighting and shadows affect what you see on film.

WHAT ARE GRIPS, GAFFERS, AND LIGHTING TECHNICIANS?

Grips, gaffers, and dolly grips. Tools? Characters in the latest sci-fi adventure? Not exactly. Grips, gaffers, and dolly grips are some of the behind-the-scenes people working in concerts, movies, and music videos.

The **grip** is responsible for placement of lights and cameras on a set or stage. It sounds simple, but it can be fairly complicated. Suppose the director of a music video wants to film a high-speed car chase. The grip would have to construct a rigging to securely attach a very expensive camera to a moving car at just the right angle to get the shot.

Before shooting begins, grips often construct platforms and scaffolding to put lights and cameras in special places.

One of the most important responsibilities of the grip is to make the set safe for the cast and crew. They make sure that the lights, scaffolding, and sets are secure. Mistakes can be costly, and if things are not secured properly, people can get hurt.

The job of the **dolly grip** is to lay the tracks that allow a dolly or crane to move during moving shots or televised productions. A dolly is a vehicle with wheels that holds a camera and camera crew.

The **key grip** manages the other grips on the set and works closely with the director of photography.

Grips do not need any special education, but they must be physically strong, handy with tools, and know something about working with electricity. They must be able to work quickly and stay two steps ahead of what is happening onstage.

There is no such thing as a normal workweek for a grip. A grip may only work two or three days a week but might work 18 or 20 hours on the days that he or she does work. Almost all grip jobs are gotten by word of mouth, so good contacts are crucial. Internships or apprenticeships are often how a grip gets started in this profession.

Where a grip's job ends, the job of **gaffer** begins. A gaffer's role is to develop and execute lighting plans for different kinds of productions. Gaffers are sometimes referred to as lighting designers. A talented gaffer can achieve all kinds of moods and many special effects using lights.

A gaffer has to consider how lights will interact with other aspects of a production and place lights so that everyone and everything is bathed in just the right amount of light. Gaffers work with other lighting technicians to set up and operate the lighting equipment during a production. They may also be responsible for supplying electricity to the set.

Gaffers and lighting technicians must have solid knowledge of electricity. Something as simple as a blown fuse, when not handled properly, can shut down a production and waste a lot of money. Mood and timing are everything in successfully lighting a stage. Every performance requires 100 percent attention to keep the lights in sync with what's happening onstage.

A good gaffer is detail oriented, flexible, and safety conscious. People skills are helpful as well, since gaffers often supervise other lighting technicians.

In addition to lighting the way for concerts and theater productions, gaffers may also light up movies, television shows, and music videos. They may work in studios or in front of live audiences. Just like in the film and video industry, the lights have to be placed for optimal effect, and towers and scaffolding have to be built.

Pursuing a degree in film schools or in theater programs at a college or university is one way to prepare for these types of technical careers. However, many grips, gaffers, and lighting technicians learn on the job with internships and apprenticeships playing an important part in their training.

TRY IT OUT

LEND A HAND

Working backstage during a school production is probably one of the best ways to learn the ropes as a grip, gaffer, or lighting technician. So make yourself available and useful for every school play and musical. The School Show Page at http://www.schoolshows.demon.co.uk/resources/technical/lxguide.htm has some excellent how-to information for school show lighting.

Check out the Low Budget Filmmakers Guide at http://www.dainter.com/infocus/newhome for more tips on lighting, recording, camera work, and special effects.

Once you've mastered some basics, you may want to contact local theater and arts organizations and volunteer to work as a stagehand or with lighting. Ballet and dance companies and children's theater groups can be good places to start. You can learn a ton by watching carefully and following the instructions of experienced stagehands and lighting technicians, and you may make some contacts that will be valuable later on.

SAY CHEESE

Gather up all the lights and flashlights in the house, a camera filled with a new roll of film, and a photogenic friend. Use the lights to arrange several different kinds of scenes. Take some photos inside; take others outside. Use only natural light. Then use flash and extra lights. Experiment, experiment, experiment. When you get the film developed, look at each photograph and see what kinds of differences your lighting choices made.

WHO TURNED OUT THE LIGHTS?

You can learn lots about grips, gaffers, and lighting technicians at these websites:

- Play hangman on-line and learn some cinematography words at http://www.cinematography.com/games/hangman.asp.
- Internet Movie Database at http://www.us.imdb.com is a fun site where you can look up cast and crew (including grips, gaffers, etc.) from your favorite films. It also sponsors some fun movie and trivia games.
- Learn about the tools grips, gaffers, and lighting technicians use at http://www.backstageweb.com/links.htm.

SPOTLIGHT ON BOOKS

To dig a little deeper into the world of grips, gaffers, and lighting technicians rustle up some of these books at your local library:

———————

Box, Harry C. *Set, Lighting Technician's Handbook: Film Lighting Equipment, Practice, and Electrical Distribution.* Woburn, Mass.: Focal Press, 1997.

Glerum, Jay O. *Stage Rigging Handbook.* Carbondale, Ill.: Southern Illinois University Press, 1997.

Kelly, Karin, and Tom Edgar. *Film School Confidential: The Insider's Guide to Film Schools.* New York: Perigee, 1997.

Malkiewicz, Kris. *Film Lighting: Talks with Hollywood's Cinematographers and Gaffers.* New York: Simon & Schuster, 1992.

Moody, James L. *Concert Lighting: Techniques, Art, and Business.* Woburn, Mass.: Focal Press, 1997.

Taub, Eric. *Gaffers, Grips, and Best Boys.* New York: St. Martin's Press, 1995.

Uva, Michael G., and Sabrina Uva. *The Grip Book.* Woburn, Mass.: Focal Press, 1997.

Vasey, John. *Concert Sound and Lighting Systems.* Woburn, Mass.: Focal Press, 1999.

Walters, Graham. *Stage Lighting Step-by-Step: The Complete Guide on Setting the Stage with Light to Get Dramatic Results.* Crozet, Vir.: Betterway Publications, 1997.

———————

ON SECOND THOUGHT

Stagehands have a language all their own. It may look and sound a lot like the language you speak, but you might want to look again. Use the glossary at http://www.stld.org.uk/Glossary.htm to add new meaning to the following familiar terms:

apron	deadend
butterfly	fly
cookie	house
corkscrew	legs

CHECK IT OUT

The Entertainment Services and
   Technology Association
875 Sixth Avenue, Suite 2302
New York, New York 10001
http://www.esta.org

The International Alliance of
   Theatrical Employees, Moving
   Picture Technicians, Artists
   and Allied Crafts
1515 Broadway, Suite 601
New York, New York 10036
http://www.iatse.lm.com

Motion Picture Studio Grips
6926 Melrose Avenue
Los Angeles, California 90038
http://www.gripslocal80.com

United States Institute for
   Theater Technology, Inc.
6443 Ridings Road
Syracuse, New York 13206-1111
http://www.usitt.org

GET ACQUAINTED

John David Peters,
Technical Director

CAREER PATH

CHILDHOOD ASPIRATION: To be an architect or actor.

FIRST JOB: Painting seats and seat numbers for San Diego's Old Globe Theater.

CURRENT JOB: Production carpenter, San Diego Opera.

DOUBLE THE PLEASURE, DOUBLE THE FUN

Two interests marked John David Peters' childhood. One was architecture and the other was acting. The acting bug hit first when Peters starred in a kindergarten production and contin-ued to score those "leading man" roles throughout elementary school. But Peters remembers that he always seemed interested in building things as well.

From the time he was in middle school, Peters was using his electives and after-school activity time to pursue both interests. He took drafting classes, engineering classes, and lots of math. He also participated in school plays as much as possible. When he was 13, he started volunteering at San Diego's Old Globe Theater, which at that time produced about eight plays each winter and hosted Shakespeare festivals each summer.

A MEETING OF THE MINDS

After high school, Peters went to a local junior college that offered an exceptional drama program. The program required all students to participate in all theatrical disciplines, both acting and technical. Although he still planned to become an actor at this point, Peters discovered that he had a real knack for the technical side of things as well.

During the summers, Peters worked for the San Diego Opera helping build scenery for their scenic studio. The more he worked on the technical side, the more his talents surfaced. He realized that he stood a better chance of success in the production side of theater than he did as a performer, so he switched gears. Looking back, Peters sees this as one of life's ironic twists of fate, because this new direction was actually a perfect blend of his interests in architecture and performing.

From junior college, Peters moved on to the International School of Performing Arts to work toward a bachelor's degree in fine arts with an emphasis in technical theater. In order to pay his tuition bills, Peters was also working as a stagehand through the San Diego Stagehands Union. His summers were once again put to good use interning with a summer-stock theater and the Santa Fe Opera.

By the time Peters graduated, he had an impressive array of practical and classroom experiences.

MUSIC WORTH SEEING

Since 1977, Peters has been working for the San Diego Opera. Starting first as head carpenter, he eventually created the position he holds now, that of production carpenter. He describes his role as that of "kingpin" for solving practical and physical problems that affect the production of elaborate scenery used in opera houses all over the world. He uses words such as organizing, supervising, implementing, and presenting to describe what he does all day. He works with the heads of wardrobe, lighting, wigs and makeup, props, and electrical departments to make sure that everyone is working with the same set of priorities. Or as Peters says he ensures that everyone is "going down the same set of tracks."

The scenic studio where all this happens consists of four huge warehouses that house welding, carpentry, drapery, and painting facilities. The studio also has an inventory of the opera's rental equipment and opera sets. It's big and there is always lots going on. For instance, it's not unusual for Peters to be juggling details for several shows at a time with one show onstage, one show in rehearsal and a couple in the scenery shop. At the same time, Peters might be doing prep work for a new show or preparing a detailed archival record of an old one before it goes into storage or out for rental.

IT'S A BIG WORLD OUT THERE

Peters says that the biggest mistake kids with an interest in theater make is to think that acting is all there is to do. According to Peters, opera alone is a multibillion-dollar business, and it's only one form of entertainment. He estimates that maybe 20 or 30 percent of that income actually goes to performers. The rest is spent in support of the productions.

The truth is that very few people have the discipline, the right combination of lucky breaks, and the God-given talent to be a star. But there is a tremendous amount of opportunity for everyone else. It takes a lot of work to make a good show and every person counts.

For a virtual tour of Peters' workshop, go on-line to http://www.sdopera.com/sdoss.htm and click on the production tours icon.

Musician

WHAT IS A MUSICIAN?

Think musician. What comes to mind first? A guy wearing no shirt and blasting awesome guitar riffs at the speed of light? A favorite country and western solo performer singing and dancing in front of a packed arena? How about the latest boy band whose pictures are plastered on the cover of every teen magazine? All of the above certainly fit the bill. But don't forget opera singers, orchestra or band instrumentalists, folk singers, children's performers, and nightclub singers.

A career as a musician or singer means different things to different people. But no matter what kind of music is involved, all musicians have some things in common. Talent is, of course, the primary requirement. Some talent may be natural but taking that talent to a professional level takes a lot of practice and learning. Most musicians start learning their craft at a fairly young age and keep it up throughout their careers.

Self-discipline is another common trait of all musicians. Practice and rehearsals are part of everyday life—even when a musician would rather be doing something else. Performing the same show night after night and consistently giving it all you've got requires a great deal of self-discipline.

Thick skin is another essential asset for musicians. It takes a lot of courage to get up in front of an audience of any size.

98

Stage fright is never an excuse from giving a good performance. Rejection is also something every musician faces at one time or another. That thick skin will help it bounce right off!

New musicians can't be too picky in choosing when and where they will perform. Schools, churches, weddings, and bar mitzvahs can provide opportunities to gain performance experience and exposure. Other popular performance venues include coffeehouses, resorts, and nightclubs.

In popular and country music, many bands start out as cover bands, which means they play other people's hits. Bands that make it big eventually start performing and recording original music. Cover bands can eke out a living playing at weddings, clubs and other social events, but they often have to supplement their income with other work while they wait for their big break.

Depending on where they are in their career, musicians and singers are compensated in different ways. Musicians and singers receive fees for performing live. Performance fees cover a huge range depending on whether you are perform-ing at a child's birthday party, for a sold-out arena of scream-ing fans, or somewhere in between. Musicians who make albums with recording companies also receive royalties (which is a percentage of sales) from any records that are sold. Additional royalties are paid when a singer or band member also happens to write any of the songs recorded on the album. A popular band or performer might also sell mer-chandise like T-shirts and posters that will bring in extra income.

Another kind of professional performer is the studio musi-cian. Studio musicians are some of the best trained, most tal-ented, and least known of all musicians. They play instruments or sing backup on other artists' albums. They may also per-form music for television and radio commercials. Studio musi-cians may not get a lot of glory, but they can make a good living making music.

Career paths for musicians are as diverse as the very dif-ferent types of musicians and singers that take them. Training for an opera singer or a classical instrumentalist is going to be quite different from that of a children's entertainer or rock musician. An opera singer will need years of classical singing lessons as well as a music degree from a university or music conservatory. A rock musician may or may not have any for-mal musical training. Most rock stars get experience by play-ing in bands and practicing as much as they can.

All vocalists need to learn how to take care of their voices. Playing and singing every night can be tough on the body, so singers and musicians have to take care of themselves by eating right, getting enough sleep, and exercising.

Those serious about a career as a musician might as well start working on it now. Develop your voice and/or learn an instrument. But take the time to honestly evaluate your tal-ent and abilities and make sure to explore other options. Working as a musician or singer can be a great career choice for some. But, just because it happens to be the most obvi-ous choice for music lovers, it's not the only option.

TRY IT OUT

START A BAND

More than one famous band got its start in someone's base-ment. Get together with some of your friends who like to make music. If you need help filling out your band, there are usually listings of musicians looking for other band members posted at local music stores.

It's OK if you are still learning your instruments. Practice together. When you have learned several songs and can play well enough that you won't embarrass yourselves, try and line up some gigs at schools, weddings or other local places. A good rule of thumb is that you are ready to perform when you can proficiently play 40 songs all the way through. That adds up to four sets of 10 songs each.

SING, SING, SING!

Take every opportunity to sing or perform in public. Try out for school chorus and musical productions. If you're comfort-able enough, audition for solos. Try singing in a church choir. Many famous singers got their start singing in church.

A ROCK 'N' ROLL SCHOOL

Learn the ins and outs, ups and downs of playing in a local rock band at Rock School at http://www.rockschool.com. This site has lessons, activities, and an exam, and it is very funny.

VOCAL CHORDS

Have you ever heard anyone say "it's not what you say, it's how you say it?" That statement is especially true for singers. Singers' voices are their instruments, and they have to keep them fine-tuned. If you hope to be a singer someday, here are some vocal exercises to get your vocal chords in shape:

 ☿ Take some free on-line voice lessons at http://www. voicelesson.com/free

☼ For more professional voice training tips, visit http://www.voiceovernet.com/resources/voicecare/index.html

ON-LINE MUSIC SCHOOL

You are so lucky! All you need to get started as a musician is an instrument of choice, a computer, and a bit of a stubborn streak. Go on-line to websites such as http://www.onlinecon-servatory.com, http://mypianolessons.com, and http://www.medolus.com for some free on-line music lessons.

Why do you need that stubborn streak? To keep you with it when the going gets tough!

TONGUE AEROBICS

Improve your diction and give your tongue a good workout at these fun websites:

☼ Mr. Twister's Tricky Tongue Twisters at http://www.loiswalker.com/twister.html
☼ Tongue Twisters from A to Z at http://www.knownet.net/users/Ackley/vocabtong.html
☼ Wacky Web Tales at http://www.eduplace.com/tales/t/tongue.html

MUSICAL HODGEPODGE

While you are surfing the net, check out some of these great resources for musicians and singers.

☼ Find a comprehensive listing of university music programs throughout the world at http://www.musicstaff.com.
☼ Learn everything you ever wanted to know about being a classical singer at http://www.classicalsinger.com.
☼ HitQuarters has contact information for record companies, A & R representatives, managers, publishers, and producers at http://www.hitquarters.com.
☼ Grand Central Music at http://www.grandcentralmusic.com is an interactive site with articles, features,

reviews, products, and services of interest to working and wannabe working musicians.

☀ You will find news, business tips, and job and gig listings for musicians at http://www.busymusician.com.

☀ Link to the best music magazines at http:// bigmeteor.com/books/mag.htm.

☀ Get signed at http://www.getsigned.com is loaded with how-to information on everything from getting signed, to playing live, and booking your own tour.

☀ Bandtools' at http://www.bandtools.com main objective is to help musicians find each other. Look here if you are searching for a band or need a musician to complete your band. They also have listings of clubs, other venues, and radio stations.

☀ Find some interesting music links as well as articles, interviews, and tip sheets for musicians at http://www.zebramusic.com.

ON A CLASSICAL NOTE

If you have an interest in opera you'll want to visit these websites:

☀ Singers on the Net at http://www.operastars.com is a site for opera singers and fans.

☀ Find resources for classical musicians at http://www. cadenza.org.

A book you'll want to read is Henry W. Simon's *100 Great Operas and Their Stories* (New York: Doubleday, 1989).

MUSIC LESSONS

There are tons of great books about the music business. Check some of these titles out at your local library to get you started:

Baxter, Mark. *The Rock-n-Roll Singer's Survival Manual.* Milwaukee: Hal Leonard Publishing Corporation, 1991.

Bennett, Gloria. *Breaking Through: From Rock to Opera—The Basic Technique of Voice.* Milwaukee: Hal Leonard Publishing Corporation, 1997.

Faragher, Scott. *Making It in Country Music: An Insider's Guide to Launching or Advancing Your Career.* Secaucus, N.J.: Citadel Press, 1996.

Johnson, Maurice. *Build and Manage Your Music Career.* Milwaukee: Hal Leonard Publishing Corporation, 1999.

Kerner, Kenny. *Going Pro: Developing a Professional Career in the Music Industry.* Milwaukee: Hal Leonard Publishing Corporation, 1999.

Lineberger, Kathryn. *The Rock Band Handbook: Everything You Need to Know to Get a Band Together and Take It on the Road.* New York: Berkley Publishing Group, 1996.

CHECK IT OUT

American Federation of Musicians
1501 Broadway, Suite 600
New York, New York 10036
http://www.afm.org

American Guild of Musical Artists
1727 Broadway
New York, New York 10019
http://www.agmanatl.com

The Children's Music Network
P.O. Box 1341
Evanston, Illinois 60204-1341
http://www.cmnonline.org

Women in Music
31121 Mission Boulevard, Suite 300
Hayward, California 94544
http://www.womeninmusic.com

GET ACQUAINTED

Eddie Coker, Singer/Musician

CAREER PATH

CHILDHOOD ASPIRATION: To be a policeman.

FIRST JOB: Working on a construction crew.

CURRENT JOB: Children's entertainer.

THE JAMES BROWN OF CHILDREN'S MUSIC

Eddie Coker has earned his nickname, "The James Brown of Children's Music." James Brown is considered one of the hardest working men in show business for adults. He is a tireless performer. Coker gives more than 250 live concerts a year for children, explaining why the title fits him so well. He sings, plays guitar, dances, and goofs around with the kids.

OPERA FOR CHILDREN?

Coker got his musical start as an opera singer in college. He toured the country as a professional opera singer for 12 years. A friend turned him on to performing opera for kids when he was visiting Texas. She invited him to do a couple of shows, and he was hooked after the first one. He remembers thinking that 500 very attentive children and an enormous hug from a class of 30 second-graders beat performing for sleeping opera patrons any day.

GLOW-IN-THE-DARK AARDVARK SISTERS

Coker joined a children's opera troupe, and his career as a children's entertainer took off from there. He began writing, recording, and performing original songs. Coker's songs are upbeat, silly, entertaining, and often have a positive message for kids. He sings silly songs about purple truck-driving ducks and glow-in-the-dark aardvark sisters. And he deals with topics such as being thankful, looking at people on the inside, and preventing drug abuse. He loves writing songs that make kids laugh and that teach them something at the same time.

Coker considers himself first and foremost a performer. He loves getting kids involved in his music with dancing, jumping, and moving around. Parents often enjoy listening to Coker's music as much as the kids, and they appreciate the values he passes on to their children.

SWEATY BUSINESS

Coker admits to working very hard and says the worst part about his job is sweating a lot. He recalls recently performing at an outdoor kids' festival in Dallas with a record high temperature of 112 degrees. In addition to shows and songwriting, he still does kids' operas, songwriting workshops, and musicals. Coker records both CDs and videos.

Even though he has been performing for years, Coker still practices a lot. He has learned to be more patient with children over the years, especially since having his own. His advice to anyone considering a career as a musician can be summed up in one word: PERSEVERE.

Music Teacher

WHAT IS A MUSIC TEACHER?

If you can sing or play a musical instrument, you probably have a music teacher to thank. Music teachers teach people of all ages how to make music—with their voices, with all kinds of music instruments, and even with computers.

Some music teachers start at the beginning, teaching the basics of music to children. Schools for children of all ages— preschool through high school—often provide music education as an important part of the learning process. Since new research supports the idea that music makes you smarter, schools not only offer music as an elective for the musically inclined but many are also mixing music with other subjects to help students learn more effectively. If you look hard enough, you can find direct links from music to all kinds of subjects such as science, math, foreign language, history, physical education, philosophy, and art.

All this adds up to more opportunities for music teachers. A big part of the job focuses on teaching students how to sing, read music, and play musical instruments. In elementary schools, music teachers often present weekly music lessons to many or all of the different grades in a school. Putting together school plays or concerts can also be part of the job.

Music teachers may be asked to help other teachers enrich language arts, social studies, math, or science lessons with music.

In middle schools and high schools, music teachers get more specialized in teaching band, orchestra, and choir classes. Organizing a school's marching band and helping students prepare for different kinds of music competitions are often the responsibilities of music teachers at this level. As students become more accomplished as musicians, teachers can present more complex musical concepts for students to learn. Some classes focus on music theory and basic composition, while others get into technique and music history. All should strive to instill a lifelong love of music in their students.

Moving up the educational ladder, you'll also find music teachers in many colleges and universities. Sometimes, their job is to teach future music teachers how to teach music. Other times, they work with students to prepare them for careers as professional musicians working in symphony orchestras, the theater, or some other aspect of the music profession.

Music teachers find that different kinds of challenges come with each grade level. For instance, those who teach elementary school students must be able to make music easy and fun. Those that teach college students must be exceptional musicians with strong teaching skills.

Of course schools are not the only places where music teachers teach. Many music teachers work at music studios or stores giving private music lessons. They teach voice or offer lessons for specific instruments such as piano or guitar. Other private music teachers work out of their homes or travel to the homes of their students to provide regular instruction. This can be an attractive option for teachers looking for part-time work or a flexible schedule that allows them more time to take care of families or other personal interests.

Whether you work with preschoolers or professionals, in order to teach music, you must know music. Most music teachers, especially those who work in schools, are required to earn a college degree in music education.

Keep in mind, however, that preparing to be a music teacher requires a much earlier start than teaching other subjects. Long before they ever get to college, future music teachers are generally found in school bands and orchestras and choral groups. They must know how to play at least one instrument in order to get admitted into most, if not all, college music programs. A halfhearted interest in music won't cut it at the college level. Passion, talent, and commitment are the only valid passports into the world of music.

TRY IT OUT

TEACHER FOR A DAY

At your age, you've probably already had some experience with music teachers. Maybe it's been in the school band, orchestra, or choir. Perhaps you've taken private music lessons. Some of these musical experiences may have been better than others.

If you ever become a music teacher, how can you make sure that learning is an enjoyable experience in your classes? You will want to be one of your student's all-time favorite teachers, won't you? Give yourself a head start on the "teacher of the year" award with the following activity.

Imagine that your music teacher is going to be absent tomorrow and that she or he has left you in charge. Using a favorite song, come up with a lesson to teach your fellow students something new about music or another subject. Make sure it's fun and educational.

Some ideas to consider: making posters or songbooks, acting out the song in a skit or play, making up new words for the song in a creative writing activity, or creating a dance routine. What other ideas can you think of?

ON A MUSICAL NOTE

If you hope to hear music in your future, you'd better make sure it's part of your present. Starting now, take advantage of every opportunity to make music—in school classes and clubs, at your church or temple, with community theater groups, or even with a group of music-loving friends. Learn how to sing and how to play at least one instrument. Learn how to read music and maybe even try your hand at writing a song or two.

The Internet can help you teach yourself all about music. Here are a few especially fun websites to explore:

- ☀ Trouble with Treble, a fun way to learn about how music is written, at http://www.tldsb.on.ca/schools/huntsvilleps/99/lessons/music/index.htm
- ☀ The New York Philharmonic KidZone, featuring the composer's workshop and all kinds of puzzles and games, at http://www.nyphilkids.com
- ☀ The American Symphony Orchestra League's website especially for kids at http://www.playmusic.org
- ☀ The Piano Education Page where you can time travel to meet a famous composer or pianist among other fun activities at http://www.umn.edu/ ~loritaf/pnokids.html
- ☀ Music Notes, an interactive on-line musical experience, at http://www.library/thinkquest.org/15413
- ☀ Pipsqueaks, a site where you can create your own music, at http://www.childrensmusic.org/Pipsqueaks.html

For an interesting book on the subject of teaching yourself music, read *Practicing for Young Musicians: You Are Your Own Teacher* by Harvey R. Snitkin (Niantic, Conn.: HMS Publications, 1997).

NAME THAT INSTRUMENT!

There's nothing quite so embarrassing as a music teacher getting his or her oboes mixed up with the tubas. Don't let this happen to you! Find out all about woodwinds, strings, percussion, and brass instruments at http://www.nyphilharmon. org/education/activities/index.htm.

At this same site, you can find instructions for making all kinds of instruments from kazoos to tube trombones to your own one-person band. Here's your chance to make your own kind of music!

THE SING-ALONG CHALLENGE

Do you know your state song? If not, take the "Career Ideas for Kids Sing-Along Challenge" and learn it. You can find the words for the official state songs of all 50 states and other U.S. territories at http://www.edu-cyberpg.com/Music/statesong.html. You are on your own for the tune. Your parents or teachers may be able to help.

Once you've got it mastered, ask your teacher if you can teach it to the rest of the class or practice your teaching skills with your family or a group of friends.

CHECK IT OUT

American Music Conference
5790 Armada Drive
Carlsbad, California 92008
http://www.amc-music.com

College Music Society
202 West Spruce Street
Missoula, Montana 59802
http://www.music.org

Music Teachers National Association
441 Vine Street, Suite 505
Cincinnati, Ohio 45202-2814
http://www.mtna.org

National Association for Music Educators
1806 Robert Fulton Drive
Reston, Virginia 20191
http://www.menc.org

National Association of Teachers of Singing
2800 University Boulevard N
Jacksonville, Florida 32211
http://www.nats.org

GET ACQUAINTED

Preston Bailey, Music Teacher

CAREER PATH

CHILDHOOD ASPIRATION: To be a beach bum.

FIRST JOB: Bagging groceries and stocking shelves at the local market.

CURRENT JOB: Music director at Petaluma Junior High School.

A MUSICAL LIFE

Preston Bailey is first to admit that he's not your typical music teacher. Music teachers usually fall in love with music as a child or teenager, graduate from high school, major in music in college, and start teaching. It started out that way for Bailey. By the age of five or six he was learning to play the guitar, he played in the school band throughout middle school and high school, and he even went to college to study music.

But, much as he loved music, Bailey discovered that he wasn't ready to be a good college student. He was too distracted with other things. Thinking it might help to get some experience in the music industry, he decided to take a semester off from school.

That semester break stretched into 15 years. During this time, Bailey did just about everything there is to do in music. He worked in a music store, he went to Hollywood and worked as a studio musician, he trained as a sound engineer, he worked on a sound stage doing sound effects for films, he worked for a production company, and he performed with an ensemble group called Music Americana. Bailey also did a little songwriting and made a few recordings.

Somewhere along the line, he started giving a few private music lessons and realized that teaching music was a gift he wanted to share with others. However, there was a rather significant detail standing between Bailey and a career as a professional music teacher: a college degree. If Bailey were to realize this dream, he'd have to go back to college and tackle all those music courses again.

Bailey was surprised to discover that this time around he was a great student. All that music experience really paid off. Bailey says it felt like the pieces in a puzzle fitting together in his mind. It made sense. He got it. Now he could not only make music, but he understood it too.

MUSIC TEACHER FOR HIRE

By the time Bailey graduated from college, he was already teaching 34 classes a week in eight different schools as an independent contractor. With a degree in hand, it was time to make things official. This time the detail standing between Bailey and his dream was money. The school districts he wanted to work for didn't have any. Music education had been cut from the elementary school budgets.

No problem—at least not for a creative musician like Bailey. He just created a position, found partners to fund it (two high school booster clubs "investing" in future band members and the school board), and started an elementary music program from scratch. The first year Bailey worked with about 500 students at 10 different schools—each school got him for half a day once a week. Eight years later, the program had grown to include 2,500 students and four full-time teachers.

MUSIC IS WHAT YOU MAKE IT

Bailey says that his main job as a music teacher is to provide opportunities for children. He says you never know what can happen when you make music available and let kids see what they can do. Music is a challenge. Some people get it and some people don't. One of the best parts of being a music teacher is when music "clicks" for a student, especially one who has struggled with school and hasn't enjoyed much success as a student.

One of Bailey's favorite stories involves a school bully. From day one in elementary school, Bailey recalls that this angry little kid was always causing trouble. Teachers and students alike knew to watch out for this guy. When he made it to eighth grade, a strange thing happened. He discovered the trumpet. And, more important, he discovered that the more he practiced, the better he played. So he practiced at home, during recess, and after school. Whenever he had the chance, he played his trumpet. It wasn't too long before he could play the trumpet very well. He was so good that he played a solo in his very first school concert. Bailey says that there wasn't a dry eye in the house when this kid finished playing a moving rendition of "Amazing Grace."

THE BIG QUESTION

In his role as music teacher, Bailey finds that students often ask him for advice about what they should do with their lives. He responds with a question: What do you like to do and do well enough that someone will pay you to do it? Bailey figures that getting paid for doing something you want to do anyway is a great way to make a living. It works for him!

Music Therapist

SKILL SET

✔ MUSIC & DANCE

✔ TALKING

✔ SCIENCE

GO to the library and see what kinds of books you can find about music therapy.

READ *The Sandy Bottom Orchestra* by Garrison Keillor and Jenny Lind Nilsson (New York: Hyperion Press, 1996).

TRY listening to different kinds of music on the radio and compare your reactions. Relaxed and mellow? Sad? Energetic?

WHAT IS A MUSIC THERAPIST?

Music is considered a healing art. Music therapists use music to diagnose and treat a wide variety of mental and physical illnesses in people of all ages. Officially speaking, the American Music Therapy Association defines music therapy as "an established health profession using music and music activities to address physical, emotional, cognitive, and social needs of children and adults with disabilities or illnesses."

Some of the places where music therapists work include psychiatric hospitals, rehabilitation facilities, hospitals, clinics, community mental health centers, drug and alcohol treatment centers, senior centers, prisons, and schools. Each setting provides opportunities to help people with different kinds of needs. For example, therapists might work with people who are mentally ill or physically handicapped, or they may work with people who have been injured in accidents. People with learning disabilities and those who are terminally ill are other types of patients seen by music therapists.

Music therapy is used to accomplish many different goals, depending, of course, on what each patient needs. For a teenage girl with an eating disorder, music therapy might be used as part of a treatment plan to improve the girl's self-image and body awareness. For an adult struggling with drug

addiction, it might be used to help redirect negative behavior. Sometimes music therapy is used to improve communication and social skills. Other times it's used to improve a person's fine and gross motor skills (fine motor skills involve small movements like those required to write with a pencil, while gross motor skills involve big movements such as those required to run or throw a ball). Increasing creativity, unleashing imagination, and encouraging independence are often goals of music therapy programs.

One thing that all the goals have in common is that none of them are musical. It's not like a musical therapist is trying to teach a person how to play an instrument. Instead they use music to change physical, mental, emotional, and social skills and behaviors. It's almost as if the therapists are doctors using music as a medicine to help people get well.

In order to be successful, music therapists have to know about more than music to do their jobs. A college degree in music therapy is a must. Music therapy courses blend the best of music and music theory with courses in more scientific areas such as psychology, anatomy, and biology. Graduating from college is just the first step. Completing a six-month internship (where they get on-the-job experience) and passing a special exam are the next steps. Then a music therapist is certified by the American Music Therapy Association and qualified to begin his or her career.

Musically inclined people with an interest in helping others may find a perfect fit in a career as a music therapist. This is one profession that offers a chance to change the world—one person at a time.

TRY IT OUT

THE DOCTOR IS IN

Try the following activities to get just a small idea of what a music therapist does.

Suppose you are a music therapist, and one of your clients is the mother of a three-month-old baby. The mother reports that the baby is having problems settling down to sleep (and the mother has dark circles under her eyes to prove it!). You suggest that she try playing some sleep-inducing music to soothe the baby as he tries to sleep. Make a list of appropriate songs the mother might play. For ideas go on-line to http://www.kididdles.com and use their "mouseum." You may want to add specific CDs that the mother might play. See what kinds of resources you can find at http://www.amazon.com that might work some lullaby magic.

Your next patient is a second-grade girl. She's extremely shy and unsure of herself. Her teacher hopes you can use music to help boost the child's self-esteem. Go back to http://www.kididdles.com and see what kinds of songs you find to encourage this child.

MOOD MUSIC

You don't have to be a music therapist to know that music affects people's moods. Some music is bright and cheerful; other music is dark and soulful with many variations in between. Do a little experiment to see how music affects you.

Gather a radio, several pieces of blank art paper, and some crayons or markers. Start with your favorite music station. Tune in and set the volume at a comfortable level (translation:

you can hear it just fine, but your next-door neighbors can't!). While you are listening, draw a picture that reflects how the music makes you feel and what it makes you think about. Don't worry about what it looks like. It doesn't even have to look like anything in particular. Use color and strokes that illustrate what you hear.

Repeat this process as you listen to a variety of different stations. Try classical music, jazz, country, oldies—a little bit of everything. Each time, make a new picture. When you are finished, compare the results. Ask your parent or a friend to try to match each picture to the type of music you were listening to.

KARAOKE CHARADES

Here's an idea to try with a group of friends. First, use scraps of paper to write words that describe every emotion you can think of: happy, sad, angry, etc. Fold papers in half and place in a bowl. Now have each person take a turn drawing an emotional cue from the bowl and singing a song that matches the mood listed on the paper. If the person gets stuck, he or she can ask for help from one person in the audience. If all else fails, the singer can sing any song in a way that conveys the mood. It's up to the audience to guess which emotion is being acted out.

DR. DJ

Your best friend is sick or your parent is stressed-out. What can you do to help? Gather up some of your favorite soothing CDs, find a comfortable place for your friend or parent to sit back and relax, and create a soothing concert for one. You don't even have to say anything. Just play several songs that will give the person a chance to unwind and get lost in the sound.

Make sure you do your homework first. Find selections that are sure to soothe and decide the most pleasing order to play them. If the goal is to help the person sleep, keep things light. If you want to cheer the person up, pick songs with some energy and fun lyrics.

CHECK IT OUT

National Association for Music Therapy
8455 Colesville Road, Suite 1000
Silver Spring, Maryland 20910
http://www.namt.com

GET ACQUAINTED

Laura Cochran,
Music Therapist

CAREER PATH

CHILDHOOD ASPIRATION:
Toyed with ideas as varied as firefighter and dancer.

FIRST JOB: Worked in a deli for eight years.

CURRENT JOB: Board Certified Music Therapist with Triangle Music Therapy, Inc.

A MUSICAL SELECTION

Music was always a big deal for Laura Cochran. By the time she started high school, she played the piano well enough to seriously consider becoming a performer. However, a little research convinced her that the competitive nature of the profession was something she could gladly do without. Both her parents were teachers, so they encouraged her to channel her musical talent into teaching, but Cochran knew that teaching wasn't quite what she was looking for either. She found her future after reading a magazine article about music therapy. She was a high school sophomore at the time, and she knew she had found the perfect career. Music therapy was it.

Now, after college, internships, board certification, and all kinds of experience as a music therapist, Cochran believes music therapy is still it. Cochran says she is exactly where she wants to be with her career. Work never feels like a waste of time, and she enjoys touching people in a way that other people can't.

A DAY IN THE LIFE OF A MUSIC THERAPIST

Cochran works as a contract music therapist, which means she works in a variety of places with a variety of populations using music as a tool to reach nonmusical goals. Since she typically works with 120–140 clients each week, she spends lots of time in her car getting from one place to the other. Which is OK. It gives her time to switch gears between one group and the next.

One stop could involve a group of elderly Alzheimer's patients in a nursing home. There the goal might be to get patients to interact with each other. Cochran always starts the session with a "hello" song that encourages her "singers" to reach out and shake hands with someone else. That alone can be a big step for some of these patients. Music can give them a glimpse of the people they used to be before Alzheimer's took over their brains.

Another stop might be at a physical rehabilitation facility where Cochran would work one-on-one with several patients. She might use instruments and action songs to help patients resume the activities of daily life.

Next on the schedule might be going into a private home to work with an autistic child or a group home where music is used to help patients who are struggling with mental illnesses or developmental disabilities. Here music is used to augment traditional types of therapy such as occupational or physical therapies.

This day may end with Cochran giving a presentation at a local hospital about how music therapy works. Other days may find Cochran rushing to a college campus to take continuing education course about new trends in the profession.

FAMILY COMES FIRST

Although there's no time to get bored in Cochran's schedule, there's always time for family. Cochran has two young children at home and finds that music and mothering is a good mix. She says music is a big part of their home life. They have songs for everything—cleaning up, going to bed, even brushing their teeth! Since Cochran plays the piano, guitar, all kinds of rhythm and percussion instruments, and sings, it's almost like having a one-mom band at home.

FUTURE MUSIC THERAPISTS BEWARE!

According to Cochran, music therapy is not a good choice for someone looking for a sit-at-a-desk and take-it-easy kind of job. This work is best suited for high-energy, physically active types. Cochran says that ideal music therapists know how to make things happen. They tend to be kind of "out there" in a way that allows them to just let loose and enjoy all kinds of people and situations. Of course, musical talent is a must, and creativity never hurts.

Music Video Producer

SKILL SET

✔ MUSIC & DANCE

✔ ART

✔ MONEY

WHAT IS A MUSIC VIDEO PRODUCER?

You love music, but you can't sing a note? The only instrument you know how to play is the stereo? Maybe that's a little extreme. Let's just say that, for whatever reason, you're looking for a career in music that doesn't require you to perform. If that's the case, music video producer is an interesting career to consider. Music video producers are the creative minds behind the videos that showcase those hot (and not so hot) new songs and artists. Hired by various record labels, television stations, or artists to make videos, the music video producer is responsible for making sure all the pieces get put together in just the right way, in exactly the right time, at exactly the right cost.

Part manager, part creative genius, part technician—that pretty much sums up what this job is all about. On the management side, the first thing that often comes up is the budget. Record labels often provide details about what they want and ask producers to tell them how much it will cost to get it. To calculate the costs, the music video producer takes the "treatment" (a script of sorts, usually written by the director) and develops a realistic and accurate budget. This money manager role continues throughout a project because the producer has to make sure that the project stays on budget. That sometimes requires tough decisions and saying no to last-minute special effects and expensive overtime costs. Keeping everything on track is one of the producer's biggest jobs.

With the money and scheduling taken care of, the producer then becomes the "creative genius." It's time to make a video! There are the location and backgrounds to scout out. Permission to use various facilities has to be obtained (especially when the producer wants to use a public place). Cast and crew have to be hired. Lights, cameras, costumes, props, and other technical equipment have to be secured and transported to the location. Success is in the details and putting them together in ways that result in a top-notch production.

The role of technician takes over on the day (or days) of the shoot. That's when the producer keeps busy supervising sound, lighting, and recording crews. After the video has been shot, the producer will supervise its postproduction including the developing of the film and the editing of the video. The producer works with directors and film editors at this point to make sure the final cut is all that it's supposed to be.

Some music video producers also act as directors of a shoot—either by choice or by necessity when working on low-budget productions. It can be tricky to keep a director's creative vision for a song in check with the realities of a budget. For instance, while a director might long to film part of the video at dusk on a beach in Tahiti, budgetary constraints may call for some creative camera work at a local swimming hole. Fortunately, this kind of situation becomes less of a problem and more of a creative opportunity for a seasoned producer.

The career path of a music video producer is similar to that of a commercial, television, or film producer. In fact, these fields tend to overlap quite a bit. A production company that makes music videos may also produce commercials or informational videos. Many music video producers go on to produce television or feature films.

Different routes will get you to a career as a music video producer. One approach would be getting a college degree in a subject such as film production or theater arts. Another approach is to find an apprenticeship at a film production company. There you'd have the equipment and opportunity you'd need for some on-the-job training. Some music video producers learn the ropes on their own by experimenting with ideas and developing independent projects.

No matter what the route taken, an imaginative, professional-quality "reel" is any music video producer's ticket to getting hired. A reel is a video that shows clips of a producer's best work. It's serves the same purpose as a résumé for those working in the music video industry.

TRY IT OUT

MAKE A VIDEO

Get your hands on a video camera—beg, borrow, or rent. Then find a music group that's willing to "perform" a little for your first video production. A few friends in a band would work. So would a school band or church choir. Select a song and write a treatment. Give everyone their cues and go through a few practice rounds. When everyone is ready, it's time to speak three powerful words: "lights, camera, action."

PHOTO BUG

Developing an eye for creating interesting and visually appealing scenes is a learned trait. You can get plenty of practice by volunteering to serve as official camera operator at school athletic games and drama productions or even various family functions. Experiment with different types of shots and angles to build your skills and comfort level behind a camera.

BEHIND THE SCENES

Learn how some of your favorite movie videos were made at http://www.futureffects.com. This website is loaded with interesting and informative articles and interviews with the people who are making some of the hottest videos around. You can also post your music video questions on their bulletin board and have them answered by working music video professionals.

Here are other websites of note:

- Watch music videos right on your computer screen at http://www.launch.com.
- Visit MTV at http://www.mtv.com.
- Visit VH1 at http://www.vh1.com.
- Find career guidance as well as links to film schools, internships, classes, and workshops at http://www. creativeplanet.com.
- Directors World at http://www.directorsworld.com often features articles about music video productions.
- Webmovie.com, the producer's guide to the web at http://www.webmovie.com, is a comprehensive site that has thousands of links to resources that music video producers utilize daily.
- Browse a list with links to production companies that make music videos at http://www.musicvideo. about.com/musicperform/musicvideo/msub7b.htm.

THE PROS AT WORK

Watch how the pros get the job done during MTV's "Making the Video" segments. These broadcasts take you behind the scenes and show you how popular videos were made. You can check out the website at http://www.mtv.com to find out days and times for local viewing. Just a note of caution here: Use discretion in choosing which videos you watch. Some videos produced by MTV, sad to say, are simply not appropriate for kids to watch.

A FEW WORDS ABOUT MUSIC VIDEO PRODUCTION

Visit the library and pick up a few of these books to find out more about careers in the music video industry:

Cartwright, Steve R. *Preproduction Planning for Video, Film, and Multimedia.* Woburn, Mass.: Focal Press, 1996.

Gates, Richard. *Production Management for Film and Video.* Woburn, Mass.: Focal Press, 1999.

Horwin, Michael. *Careers in Film and Video Production.* Woburn, Mass.: Focal Press, 1990.

Jacobs, Robert M. *The Independent Video Producer: Establishing a Profitable Video Business.* Woburn, Mass.: Focal Press, 1999.

Kleiler, David, and Robert Moses. *You Stand There: Making Music Video.* New York: Three Rivers Press, 1997.

Lyver, Des, and Graham Swainson. *Basics of Video Production.* Woburn, Mass.: Focal Press, 1999.

Noronha, Shonan F. R. *Opportunities in Television and Video Careers.* Lincolnwood, Ill.: VGM Horizons, 1993.

Reiss, Steven, Neil Feineman, Jeff Ayeroff, and Michael Stipe. *Thirty Frames per Second: The Visionary Art of the Music Video.* New York: Harry N. Abrams, Inc., 2000.

Roth, Cliff. *The Low Budget Video Bible: The Essential Do-It-Yourself Guide to Making Top Notch Video on a Shoestring Budget.* New York: Desktop Video Systems, 1995.

Shyles, Leonard. *Video Production Handbook.* New York: Houghton Mifflin, 1998.

CHECK IT OUT

American Association of
  Producers
15030 Ventura Boulevard,
  Suite 675
Sherman Oaks, California 91403
http://www.tvproducers.org

Independent Feature Project
1964 Westwood Boulevard,
  Suite 205
Los Angeles, California 90025
http://www.ifp.org

Music Video Production
  Association

940 North Orange Drive,
  Suite 104
Hollywood, California 90038
http://www.mvpa.com

Producers Guild of America
400 South Beverly Drive
Beverly Hills, California 90212
http://www.producersguild.com

Society of Motion Picture and
  Television Engineers
595 West Hartsdale Avenue
White Plains, New York 10607
http://www.smpte.org

GET ACQUAINTED

Gigi Greco,
Music Video Producer

CAREER PATH

CHILDHOOD ASPIRATION: To
be a veterinarian.

FIRST JOB: Runway model when
she was seven years old.

CURRENT JOB: Owner and president of Art Attack Productions,
Inc., a music video production
company.

A PICTURE'S WORTH A THOUSAND WORDS

Gigi Greco seemed destined for a career as a veterinarian
when she was a child. She took in every stray bird, cat, and
dog she found—or that somehow seemed to find her.

By the time she went to college, she was all set for a career as a writer. Along with pursuing a degree in journalism, Greco says she was a regular contributor to several campus "rags" (free magazines). She wrote mostly about music—interviewing bands that came to town, reviewing albums, critiquing concerts, and such.

Greco was sailing along, doing well in her classes, and enjoying the work when two words from a respected professor stopped her short. He told that her writing was "overly descriptive" and said she was trying too hard to describe every aspect of her stories, even those that readers should be free to imagine on their own.

Greco realized that he was right but so was she. She was descriptive on purpose. She wanted to paint vivid pictures with her work. What she really wanted to do was "show stories, not just tell them." That's when Greco switched her major from journalism to radio, television, and film. Then she hit the streets of New York with a video camera.

ME AND MY BIG MOUTH

One of Greco's first jobs was working as a personal assistant to a director for Mondo TV in New York. The job was short-lived, however, because the director threw her off the set when he overhead her telling someone how she could have shot a scene better. He promised her that she would never work again in that city, but he was wrong. In fact, Greco remembers with pleasure the day he wandered onto a street where she was shooting a commercial for a client and she got to order him off her set! They both had a good laugh about the turn of events.

ART ATTACK!

From New York, Greco went to Nashville where she landed a great job producing television commercials. The commercials were put into syndication, so they aired all over the country. This gave Greco's work some great airtime.

When Greco and her husband moved to Austin, Texas, Greco decided it was time to start her own music video production company. Now she works with recording artists and record labels representing all kinds of music genres—alternative, country, Tejano, hip-hop, Christian, and pop.

As producer and director of a wide variety of music video projects, Greco has found the perfect niche for "showing her stories." Many projects start as a blank slate. In this case, Greco listens to a song and develops a story around her impressions of the music. According to Greco, the beauty of music videos is that you can do anything you want.

PUTTING IT ALL TOGETHER

A music video can take as long as a month to produce. The process starts by writing a treatment or script for the video. Sometimes a client also likes to see storyboards that illustrate each scene and concept in the video. Then there are the inevitable changes and revisions as Greco works out the kinks with the client. Next comes casting the performers and scouting locations for the shoot. Finding out as much as possible about the artists is another important part of Greco's background research. Then there are more details to take care of—crew to hire, equipment to acquire and organize, meals to order for the day of the shoot, etc. A big part of the preparation process is building or dressing the set where the video will be filmed. After all this is done, it's finally time to shoot the video. Then Greco says she is constantly watching the clock and the camera to make sure they aren't wasting time or film and are getting everything they need on tape.

There's still plenty to do once the video itself has been made. Technical things such as film transfers and color corrections happen first. Editing the tape can take several days to get everything just right. Finally comes the best part of all: seeing the video played on television stations. That's when lots of people get to "see" Greco's stories.

A WORD TO THE WISE

Greco has news for you. She says that you can do anything you want to do and don't let anyone tell you otherwise. If you have a dream, follow it!

Recording Executive

SKILL SET

✔ MUSIC & DANCE

✔ TALKING

✔ MONEY

WHAT IS A RECORDING EXECUTIVE?

Does hanging out with famous rock stars, attending glamorous parties with the movers and shakers of the music industry, and personally shaping the course of popular music sound exciting to you? How about spending an evening in a smoke-filled nightclub listening to a lousy band because someone told you they were sure to become the next hot act? Both scenarios come with the territory for many recording executives.

The bottom line is that recording executives make and sell music. Sounds easy enough. But, it takes a lot of hard work and music business know-how to keep those hits coming.

There are basically two kinds of recording executives; those who work for major record labels and those who work on their own as independent music producers. Some, but not all, music executives tend to work with a particular kind of music such as rock, pop, classical, jazz, or country.

Executives are responsible for getting new recordings out where music fans can buy them. Depending on their job titles, executives might be responsible for some or all of the tasks that it takes to get this job done. In any case, recording executives are only as successful as their latest recordings. That's why one of the most important parts of this job is staying current with the latest trends or, better yet, staying one step ahead of the next big trend. The most successful executives are those who can accurately predict what their audiences want to hear both today and next month. Count on this aspect of the business to add more than a little excitement and tension to the job.

As far as the nitty-gritty aspects of the job go, recording executives do things such as scout out new talent, select new songs, make arrangements for studio recording time, hire sound engineers and studio technicians, and find just the right mix of background musicians and vocalists. All that's just to get a CD produced. Developing and implementing marketing and promotional campaigns to sell the recordings also fall under an executive's responsibilities.

In larger companies a team of executives assumes many of these roles. Their job titles might include:

A & R representatives (which stands for artist and repertoire) or talent scouts. Their job is to find and sign talented new musicians and groups. They're also always on the lookout for great new songs for their artists to sing. You can often spot

A & R reps by the piles of demo tapes piled up on their desks. Aspiring musicians and songwriters looking for lucky breaks send in their tapes.

A & R jobs are tough to get and even tougher to keep. A & R reps must continually prove themselves by signing new, marketable talent. The best route to an A & R job is to take any job at a record label and work your way up. Most A & R reps are promoted from within.

Record producers develop the sound and produce albums for their record label. The producer handles all the details (and there are many) of getting a record made. Over time, they develop excellent contacts in the business and gain access to the best engineers, studio musicians, and technicians for each project.

Marketing, promotions, and sales executives take over once a record has been recorded, mixed, mastered, and duplicated. These executives are responsible for getting the word out about new recordings and making it easy for people to buy them.

The number-one job for the promotions executives is getting the company's songs played on the radio. They work with disc jockeys and program managers at radio stations around the country. They introduce their label's new releases to the radio stations, provide them with promotional materials, and do whatever it takes to get airplay, which generally includes plenty of socializing, schmoozing, and cajoling.

Independents (indies) operate much differently. In fact, at a small independent label, the producer may be responsible for everything from discovering talent to promoting the album after it's made.

How does a person become a recording executive? It depends. Success is often a blend of education, experience, and a little luck. Useful college degrees include business, music management, marketing, or communications. The best assets for this career track are an ear for music and a head for business.

Although a college degree is definitely an asset when looking for a job with a record label, it would be unusual for a recent college grad to land an executive position. Most executives start with a low-level, low-paying job just to get in the door. Many find that a college internship provides just the right "in" for landing a job after graduation. Those that make the climb to the top are the ones who learn fast, work hard, and prove themselves to be innovative and responsible leaders.

TRY IT OUT

PICK THE HITS

Billboard magazine has an awesome on-line game in which you can run your own "virtual" record company. Pick the songs that you think will top the charts and see how in tune you are with the music-buying public. Take the *Billboard Challenge: The Online A & R Game* at http://challenge.billboard.com/challenge/.

DEMO SOME BANDS

Visit the new artist section at Napster (http://artist.napster.com/resources.html) and download some music by new and unknown talent. Napster is virtually open to any artist or group (good, bad, or downright awful) that is looking to get their music heard. Analyze what you hear and see if you can predict some winners. Keep a log of the new artists you liked and why. You never know. You may discover the next huge act before anyone else has even heard of them.

Another website worth visiting is TAXI at http://www.taxi.com, which connects unsigned artists and bands with record labels. The site includes some great music industry resources including entertaining and informative interviews with some music industry insiders.

THE MUSIC MAJORS

Following are web addresses for some of the major recording labels:

☼ http://www.sonymusic.com
☼ http://www.aristarec.com
☼ http://www.amrecords.com
☼ http://virginrecords.com

For a comprehensive list of additional record labels visit http://www.bandlink.com. Visit several to compare the stars and songs they represent. Which one(s) represent your favorite artists? Which one would you most like to work for someday?

ON-LINE EXECUTIVES

The following websites are where real recording executives go for the latest news about the music industry. Find out what you can about current affairs in music. And remember, it's not just what you know, it's what you do with what you know.

☼ Visit *Billboard* magazine's site at http://www.billboard.com to take a peek at the charts and for all the music industry buzz.
☼ Pro and Home Recording Resources on the Internet at http://www.prorec.com has some great resources including interviews from the recording end of the music business.
☼ The Recording Website at http://www.recordingwebsite.com is a more technical site on the ins and outs of recording music.
☼ The Musicians Resource Page at http://www2.bitstream.net/~weis0205/musicresource2.html is a good place to search for more information on the music business.
☼ Indiecentre at http://www.indiecentre.com is a site that helps independent artists get their music out. It has information on everything from starting your own label to mastering, promoting, and touring.

DO-IT-YOURSELF PRODUCTIONS

Get the gang together to make your own recording! Ask around to find some musically inclined classmates. Invite them over or arrange to meet somewhere to record them making music. Chances are they'll be flattered and will be happy to play along in your very first recording production. Check out websites linked to http://www.homerecording. about.com/musicperform/homerecording or http://www. homerecording.com for some helpful home recording tips.

Or try some of the tips found in this book:

McLan, Peter, and Larry Wichman. *Musician's Guide to Home Recording: How to Make Great Recordings at Home.* New York: Music Sales Corp., 1994.

FOR THE RECORD

Visit the library and pick up a few of these books to find out more about what it takes to be a music producer and what it takes to produce music:

Burgess, Richard James. *Art of Record Production.* New York: Omnibus Press, 1998.

Kennedy, Rick, and Randy McNutt. *Little Labels—Big Sound: Small Record Companies and the Rise of American Music.* Bloomington: Indiana University Press, 1999.

Mellor, David. *How to Become a Record Producer.* Carle Place, N.Y.: Cimino Publishing Group, 1997.

Pettigrew, Jim. *The Billboard to Music Publicity.* New York: Watson-Guptill Publishing, 1997.

CHECK IT OUT

Music Publisher's Association
PMB 246
1562 First Avenue

New York, New York 10028
http://www.mpa.org

National Association of Record Industry Professionals
5757 Wilshire Boulevard
Museum Square, Suite 440
Los Angeles, California 90036-3684
http://narip.com

National Association of Recording Merchandisers
9 Eves Drive, Suite 120
Marlton, New Jersey 08053
http://narm.com

Recording Industry Association of America
1330 Connecticut Avenue NW, Suite 300
Washington, D.C. 20036
http://www.riaa.com

GET ACQUAINTED

Derek Jones,
Recording Executive

CAREER PATH

CHILDHOOD ASPIRATION: To be a television journalist.

FIRST JOB: Waiter for a friend's catering company.

CURRENT JOB: Director of media relations and promotions at Rocketown Records.

AN EARLY START

Derek Jones began exploring his career options at an early age. He wanted to be a television anchorman, so he recruited some friends to set up a video camera and tape newscasts complete with weather and sports. Now grown up, Jones continues a revised version of that early tradition in his role as director of media relations and promotions for a record production company.

FRIENDS IN HIGH PLACES

Contemporary recording artist Michael W. Smith is an old family friend from Jones' hometown. Jones' family were frequent guests of the Smiths' in Nashville and had some of the best seats in the house for some of Smith's earliest performances. Jones recalls forming an instant fascination with Nashville—especially the thriving music industry.

One summer during high school, Jones filled in as Smith's personal assistant and loved the job! After graduating from a small high school in West Virginia, Jones moved to Nashville to attend Belmont University and became Smith's personal assistant during his college years. The education, coupled with this experience, was great preparation for his current job.

About the time Jones graduated from college with a degree in music business, his mentor and boss, Smith, was starting a new record label called Rocketown Records. Jones was offered a job with the new company and, realizing it was a great opportunity, he accepted.

THE "GO-TO" GUY

Derek says there is no such thing as a typical day on the job for him. He spends tons of time on the phone and on-line answering emails. He has two main areas of responsibility: radio and publicity. On the radio side, Jones calls about 75 radio stations each week to make sure they are playing Rocketown's songs. He chooses singles from Rocketown albums, edits them, and mails them out with fun promotional and giveaway items to radio stations all over the world. Radio program directors everywhere know that Jones is the guy to go to when they need good music.

The publicity side of Jones' job requires even more talking. He sends out press packets and information (music and videos) for Rocketown's artists and then pitches story ideas to magazines, newspapers, and TV shows. He arranges interviews for the label's artists, and he writes press releases and biographies. Jones is also the official spokesperson for the label, so he fields informational calls, organizes press conferences, and attends award shows.

NEVER A DULL MOMENT

Jones' incredible job is even more enjoyable because of the people he works with—both coworkers and artists. Doing the job right involves building good relationships with all kinds of people. Jones has a lot of fun meeting people on the road during promotional and concert tours and keeping in touch with all his radio and publicity friends.

If there were a downside to the job, it's the hours. They can get long, and Jones admits that he often overextends himself. But, Jones says, it's definitely worth it.

SOME SAGE ADVICE

Jones has a little advice for kids who may really want to do something but feel they don't have the right kind of experience or know-how. The advice is this: Jump in and do it. You'll learn even if you make some mistakes, and chances are that when you're doing something you really want to do, you won't mind working extra hard to succeed.

Oh, and one more thing. Jones says to take good care of your friends. You never know where those friendships might lead in your future. He never expected his entire career to revolve around an old family friend. But he sure is glad he had a good relationship with Michael W. Smith.

You can learn more about Jones and Rocketown Records at http://www.rocketownrecords.com.

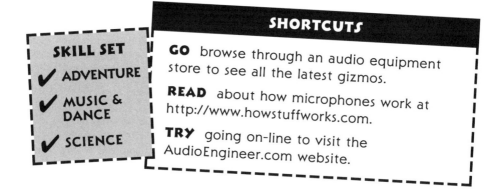

WHAT IS A SOUND ENGINEER?

Music and dance are meant to be seen *and* heard. The hearing part is achieved, in part, due to the work of sound engineers. Sound engineers operate elaborate, high-tech sound equipment to capture music and other sounds in just the right way. Their job is to amplify, enhance, record, mix, or reproduce sound in all kinds of performing arts situations.

It's not as easy as pushing a record button. Sound engineers work with all kinds of amplifiers, microphones, tuners, receivers, digital audio systems, turntables, pickups, digital recorders, and speaker systems. They operate all kinds of controls to maintain correct sound levels. Have you ever seen the cockpit of an airplane? A sound engineer's control room is similar in terms of the number of levers and gadgets there are to keep up with.

Sound engineers listen for things most people never think about in a recording, let alone hear. One thing sound engineers concern themselves with is background noise. No one really wants to pay to hear sniffling, rustling paper, or other distracting noises on a recording, so studio engineers use special techniques to isolate the right sounds and eliminate the wrong ones.

If you ever happen by a sound studio while a recording is in session, you are likely to see a big sign that says "QUIET.

Sound Engineer

Recording in progress." The goal is to get the recording environment so quiet that you really can hear a pin drop. Of
course, that's only before the music starts!

Another consideration that sound engineers work with is
acoustics. This has a lot to do with the environment itself—
the design of the space, the height of the ceiling, the thick-
ness of the walls, etc. All these things factor in to how sound
sounds. Acoustics is somewhat of a science in itself, and some
sound engineers actually become experts in this area alone.

Sound engineers work in recording and television studios as
well as in any situation requiring sound equipment. Such
places include concert halls, auditoriums, sports arenas, large
churches and synagogues, lecture halls, and the like. Some
work is done in soundproof sound studios while other work is
done amid crowds of people in indoor and outdoor facilities.

Apprenticeship and internship opportunities have long
played a big role in training for sound engineers. However, as
technology gets more complicated, formal training is often
seen as a good supplement for on-the-job training. Training
in sound engineering or electronics can be found at many

vocational technical schools. Engineers who choose to specialize in one of the more complex aspects of the field—such as equipment design and manufacture—may opt for a full-fledged college degree in a field such as electrical engineering.

Whatever the educational path, the fact is that sound engineers never really stop learning. New equipment and techniques are developed all the time, and there are always new sound situations and challenges to deal with. Sound engineers need to be prepared to stay current on the latest innovations.

TRY IT OUT

ON-LINE NOISE

The Web is a good source for information about the latest happenings in the sound business. There are a few websites where you'll find some fun and lots of technical information about things related to this profession. One good example is Webnoize, a source of news about the movers and shakers of the entertainment side of sound, at http://www.webnoize. com.

WE'VE COME A LONG WAY, BABY

You'll be able to appreciate modern technology better once you've seen what it's replaced. For an interesting blast to the past, visit a website that explores the world's earliest television recordings at http://www.dfm.dircon.co.uk.

Compare what you learn here with what you can find out about the latest technology by doing an on-line search for audio equipment or recording techniques or by visiting an audio equipment store. For some on-line shopping, try these websites for giants in the sound industry:

- ☼ http://www.bose.com
- ☼ http://www.dolby.com
- ☼ http://www.sony.com

AN INSIDE JOB

Get hands-on experience with some of these fun electronic kits, all of which are available for purchase through http://www.etoys.com or a local toy store:

- ☀ *Room Alarm,* made by Scientific Explorer, lets you build your own private alarm system (guaranteed to scare the pants off your nosy siblings!) while you explore the teeny, tiny world of electrons, protons, and neutrons.
- ☀ *30 in One Electronic Project Lab,* by Small World Toys, offers all kinds of "electrifying" activities.
- ☀ *Logiblocks: Mega Bloc Set,* by Action Product, gives electronic whiz kids a chance to build a "city" full of security gadgets such as burglar alarms, water sensors, Morse code systems, and more.

Once you're ready for more sophisticated stuff, take a look at RadioShack's on-line catalog at http://www.radioshack.com/. Look under electronic kits for projects that take you from simple all the way to advanced.

THE SCIENCE OF SOUND

Find out the hows and whys of sound and electronic processes by setting up your own sound lab at home. Here are books full of experiences for the scientist lurking within:

———

VanCleave, Janice. *Electricity: Mind-boggling Experiments You Can Turn Into Science Fair Projects.* New York: John Wiley & Sons, 1994.

———. *Physics for Every Kid: 101 Easy Experiments in Motion, Heat, Light, Machines, and Sound.* New York: John Wiley & Sons, 1991.

Wood, Robert. *Electricity and Magnetism Fundamentals: Funtastic Science Activities for Kids.* New York: McGraw Hill, 1996.

———. *Sound Fundamentals: Funtastic Science Activities for Kids.* New York: McGraw Hill, 1997.

———

JOIN THE CLUB

The Society of Broadcast Engineers (SBE) sponsors a program for high school students who are interested in broadcast engineering. Once you are in at least ninth grade, you can join and become eligible for a number of free resources. You'll get opportunities to learn about communications technology such as computers, transmitters, and audio and video equipment. For more information go on-line to http://www.sbe.org/youth?membership.htm or contact the Society of Broadcast Engineers at the address below.

CHECK IT OUT

Audio Engineering Society
60 East 42nd Street, Room 2520
New York, New York 10165
http://www.aes.org

National Academy of Recording Arts and Sciences
3402 Pico Boulevard
Santa Monica, California 90405
http://www.grammy.org

Society of Broadcast Engineers
8445 Keystone Crossing, Suite 140
Indianapolis, Indiana 46240
http://www.sbe.org

Society of Motion Picture and Television Engineers
595 West Hartsdale Avenue
White Plains, New York 10607
http://www.smpte.org

Society of Professional Audio Recording Services
4300 10th Avenue North
Lake Worth, Florida 33461
http://www.spars.com

GET ACQUAINTED

Michael Tarsia,
Sound Engineer

CAREER PATH

CHILDHOOD ASPIRATION: To be a lawyer.

FIRST JOB: Telephone salesperson for the blind.

CURRENT JOB: President of Sigma Sound Services, Inc.

A HEAD START

Michael Tarsia has been working in sound studios since he was four years old. That's how old he was when he watched his father work as an engineer at a small neighborhood studio. As he grew up, so did his father's business. His father eventually started his own studio (the same one Tarsia runs now) and became one of the most famous sound engineers in the business.

As a boy, Tarsia spent most of his summers hanging out at the studio. By the time he graduated from high school, he'd pretty much done it all: starting as a gofer, working as a receptionist, driving the company van, cleaning up the studios. You name it and he's probably done it. He also picked up some of the technical aspects of the business by watching the engineers do their jobs.

Even with all that, or maybe because of it, Tarsia really didn't plan to follow in his father's footsteps. He went to college with the intention of becoming a lawyer. But then he discovered that what real attorneys do and what TV lawyers do are two different things. That was enough to convince Tarsia that the legal profession wasn't a good fit for him. He'd had visions of brilliantly arguing cases in court without realizing that for every hour an attorney spends in court he probably spends 100 in the library doing research.

Tarsia admits feeling a bit lost and unsure of what to do with himself at that point, but he completed his college education and earned a degree in English and philosophy. After graduating, he went back to the studio and started working as an assistant. He eventually started running sessions of his own and soon developed a style of his own—quick and comfortable—that clients liked.

IT'S ALL IN THE MIND

After a couple of decades in the business, Tarsia has built quite a reputation for himself. Since his dad started the studio in 1969, Sigma Sound has earned more than 150 gold and platinum awards and has worked with famous stars such as Madonna, Billy Joel, and David Bowie. Tarsia even won a Grammy award in 1990 in recognition for his work on Patti LaBelle's Grammy-winning album called *Burnin'*. He took over as president of the company in 1990, although he says he still prefers working in the studio to running the show.

Tarsia credits his success with two things in particular. One is the ability to "get inside his client's minds." He's learned how to make artists feel comfortable, how to talk to artists (and when to shut up!), and how to bring out their best work. He compares this ability to the bedside manner that successful doctors have.

Technical know-how is the other special skill Tarsia uses to get the job done. Once he understands what a client wants, he uses this skill to translate their vision into sound. According to Tarsia, success in this business depends 50 percent on knowing what to say and 50 percent on talent.

A LONG DAY'S NIGHT

Another thing that clients like about Tarsia is that he's always available—even if it means working long hours or rearranging vacation plans. A case in point is a session he conducted with Patti LaBelle. She had only a few days open in her schedule and wanted to work over the July 4th weekend one year. No problem. They started working and didn't stop for 80 hours straight!

Tarsia says that, during long sessions like those, a second wind kicks in after 12 or 16 hours. Then, by the time his brain shuts off and he starts working on instinct, he does some of his best work.

Tarsia's ability to work long hours is legendary among his friends. They say that no matter how long they can stay awake, Tarsia can stay awake an hour longer!

SOLID GOLD

The music is the best part of the job for Tarsia. He says that playing a part in creating the songs he hears on the radio is better than getting a paycheck.

Tarsia advises young people who want to get into the business someday to "get their feet wet." By that he means you should experience music as much as you can. Experiment with different sounds, make recordings of friends playing music, and do anything else you can to find your special place in the music world. You may find that becoming a sound engineer is the perfect choice for you, but you may find that it's not.

Tarsia says that all the technical knowledge in the world can't replace the creative spark of talent that it takes to make it as a sound engineer. If you've got it, that's great. But if not, there are lots of other cool things to do in music. The most important thing, Tarsia believes, is that your heart is in whatever you do. That's where you'll find the greatest reward.

COMPOSE A MUSICAL DETOUR!

Careers in music and dance rock! There are so many interesting options out there. Many of you may not have considered all the options before. Many of you may not have even heard of some of them before. Check out the lists that follow and see if you can find a career that jives with what you want to do with your life.

MORE CAREERS TO SING ABOUT

ENTERTAINING OPTIONS

The ideas profiled in this book aren't the only ways to make music and dance the center of your career. Here are some more ways to land yourself right in the middle of what you love most:

dance therapist
film music editor
music copyist
music critic
music librarian

music store clerk
music store manager
singing messenger
studio musician

WITH A CREATIVE TOUCH

Here are some career ideas to help musicians and dancers look good—whether it's in printed promotional materials or onstage.

advertising artist
advertising designer
catalog illustrator
CD/record designer
costumer
photographer

production hair stylist
production makeup artist
prop designer
set designer
wardrobe mistress

ON THE BOSSY SIDE

Someone has to lead the way. Here are some careers that involve managing and directing various aspects of the artistic process.

artist and repertoire (A & R) rep
choreographer
development director
managing director
music producer

nightclub manager
resort entertainment director
royalties broadcast monitor
stage director
tour manager

JUST A FEW TECHNICALITIES

Musical instruments and equipment don't just pop up out of nowhere. The lights and sounds at a musical or dance production don't just magically appear on their own. Someone has to make them, use them, and take care of them. Below is a list of job titles for those "someones."

audio equipment manufacturer
dance apparel manufacturer
instrument manufacturer
instrument repair specialist
instrument stringer

lighting designer
piano tuner
sound equipment manager
sound mixer
synthesizer specialist

THE RIGHT MIX

If your interests and abilities are taking you in another direction, but you love music and dance too, here's one thing to remember: Anything you can do in the business world, you can do in the world of music and dance. For example, you love music and you want to be a lawyer. Why not combine the two and become a lawyer who specializes in entertainment law? Here are some other creative ways to bring what you've got and what you want into the picture:

accountant
attorney
file clerk
public relations director
marketing executive

music publisher
music software designer
personal assistant
receptionist
sales rep

INFORMATION IS POWER

Mind-boggling, isn't it? There are so many great choices, so many jobs you've never heard of before. How will you ever narrow it down to the perfect spot for you?

First, pinpoint the ideas that sound the most interesting to you. Then, find out all you can about them. As you may have noticed, a similar pattern of information was used for each of the career entries featured in this book. Each entry included:

- ☼ a general description or definition of the career
- ☼ some hands-on projects that give readers a chance to actually experience a job
- ☼ a list of organizations to contact for more information
- ☼ an interview with a professional

You can use information like this to help you determine the best career path to pursue. Since there isn't room in one book to profile all these music and dance career choices, here's your chance to do it yourself. Conduct a full investigation into a music and dance career that interests you.

Please Note: If this book does not belong to you, use a separate sheet of paper to record your responses to the following questions.

CAREER TITLE _____

WHAT IS A _____?
Use career encyclopedias and other
resources to write a description of this
career.

SKILL SET

✔ _____
✔ _____
✔ _____

TRY IT OUT
Write project ideas here. Ask your parents and your teacher
to come up with a plan.

CHECK IT OUT
List professional organizations where you can learn more
about this profession.

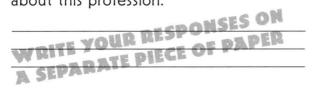

GET ACQUAINTED
Interview a professional in the field and summarize your findings.

DON'T STOP NOW!

GO FOR IT!

It's been a fast-paced trip so far. Take a break, regroup, and look at all the progress you've made.

1st Stop: Self-Discovery

You discovered some personal interests and natural abilities that you can start building a career around.

2nd Stop: Exploration

You've explored an exciting array of career opportunities in music and dance. You're now aware that your career can involve either a specialized area with many educational requirements or that it can involve a practical application of skills with a minimum of training and experience.

At this point, you've found a couple of (or few) careers that really intrigue you. Now it's time to put it all together and do all you can to make an informed, intelligent choice. It's time to move on.

3rd Stop: Experimentation

By the time you finish this section, you'll have reached one of three points in the career-planning process.

1. **Green light!** You found it. No need to look any further. This is *the* career for you. (This may happen to a lucky few. Don't worry if it hasn't happened yet for you. This whole process is about exploring options, experimenting with ideas, and, eventually, making the best choice for you.)
2. **Yellow light!** Close, but not quite. You seem to be on the right path, but you haven't nailed things down for sure. (This is where many people your age end up, and it's a good place to be. You've learned what it takes to really check things out. Hang in there. Your time will come.)
3. **Red light!** Whoa! No doubt about it, this career just isn't for you. (Congratulations! Aren't you glad you found out now and not after you'd spent four years in college preparing for this career? Your next stop: Make a U-turn and start this process over with another career.)

Here's a sneak peek at what you'll be doing in the next section.

☼ First, you'll pick a favorite career idea (or two or three).
☼ Second, you'll snoop around the library to find answers to the 10 things you've just got to know about your future career.
☼ Third, you'll pick up the phone and talk to someone whose career you admire to find out what it's really like.
☼ Fourth, you'll link up with a whole world of great information about your career idea on the Internet (it's easier than you think).
☼ Fifth, you'll go on the job to shadow a professional for a day.

Hang on to your hats and get ready to make tracks!

#1 NARROW DOWN YOUR CHOICES

You've been introduced to quite a few music and dance career ideas. You may also have some ideas of your own to add. Which ones appeal to you the most?

Write your top three choices in the spaces below. (Sorry if this is starting to sound like a broken record, but . . . **if this book does not belong to you, write your responses on a separate sheet of paper.**)

1. _____
2. _____
3. _____

WRITE YOUR RESPONSES ON A SEPARATE PIECE OF PAPER

#2 SNOOP AT THE LIBRARY

Take your list of favorite career ideas, a notebook, and a helpful adult with you to the library. When you get there, go to the reference section and ask the librarian to help you find

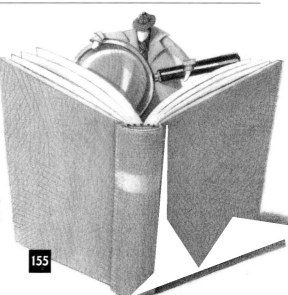

155

books about careers. Most libraries will have at least one set of career encyclopedias. Some of the larger libraries may also have career information on CD-ROM.

Gather all the information you can and use it to answer the following questions in your notebook about each of the careers on your list. Make sure to ask for help if you get stuck.

TOP 10 THINGS YOU NEED TO KNOW ABOUT YOUR CAREER

1. What kinds of skills does this job require?
2. What kind of training is required? (Compare the options for a high school degree, trade school degree, two-year degree, four-year degree, and advanced degree.)
3. What types of classes do I need to take in high school in order to be accepted into a training program?
4. What are the names of three schools or colleges where I can get the training I need?
5. Are there any apprenticeship or internship opportunities available? If so, where? If not, could I create my own opportunity? How?
6. How much money can I expect to earn as a beginner? How much with more experience?
7. What kinds of places hire people to do this kind of work?
8. What is a typical work environment like? For example, would I work in a busy office, outdoors, or in a laboratory?
9. What are some books and magazines I could read to learn more about this career? Make a list and look for them at your library.
10. Where can I write for more information? Make a list of professional associations.

#3 CHAT ON THE PHONE

Talking to a seasoned professional—someone who experiences the job day in and day out—can be a great way to get the inside story on what a career is all about. Fortunately for you, the experts in any career field can be as close as the nearest telephone.

Sure it can be a bit scary calling up an adult whom you don't know. But, two things are in your favor:

1. They can't see you. The worst thing they can do is hang up on you, so just relax and enjoy the conversation.
2. They'll probably be happy to talk to you about their job. In fact, most people will be flattered that you've called. If you happen to contact someone who seems reluctant to talk, thank them for their time and try someone else.

Here are a few pointers to help make your telephone interview a success.

- ☼ Mind your manners and speak clearly.
- ☼ Be respectful of their time and position.
- ☼ Be prepared with good questions and take notes as you talk.

One more commonsense reminder: Be careful about giving out your address and DO NOT arrange to meet anyone you don't know without your parents' supervision.

TRACKING DOWN CAREER EXPERTS

You might be wondering by now how to find someone to interview. Have no fear! It's easy, if you're persistent. All you have to do is ask. Ask the right people and you'll have a great lead in no time.

A few of the people to ask and sources to turn to are

Your parents. They may know someone (or know someone who knows someone) who has just the kind of job you're looking for.

Your friends and neighbors. You might be surprised to find out how many interesting jobs these people have when you start asking them what they (or their parents) do for a living.

Librarians. Since you've already figured out what kinds of companies employ people in your field of interest, the next step is to ask for information about local employers. Although it's a bit cumbersome to use, a big volume called *Contacts Influential* can provide this kind of information.

Professional associations. Call or write to the professional associations you discovered in Activity #1 a few pages back and ask for recommendations.

Chambers of commerce. The local chamber of commerce probably has a directory of employers, their specialties, and their phone numbers. Call the chamber, explain what you are looking for, and give the person a chance to help the future workforce.

Newspaper and magazine articles. Find an article about the subject you are interested in. Chances are pretty good that it will mention the name of at least one expert in the field. The article probably won't include the person's phone number (that would be too easy), so you'll have to look for clues. Common clues include the name of the company that the expert works for, the town that he or she lives in, and if the person is an author, the name of his or her publisher. Make a few phone calls and track the person down (if long distance calls are involved, make sure to get your parents' permission first).

INQUIRING KIDS WANT TO KNOW

Before you make the call, make a list of questions to ask. You'll cover more ground if you focus on using the five w's (and the h) that you've probably heard about in your creative writing classes: Who? What? Where? When? How? and Why? For example,

1. Who do you work for?
2. What is a typical work day like for you?
3. Where can I get some on-the-job experience?
4. When did you become a _____ ?
   (profession)
5. How much can you earn in this profession? (But, remember it's not polite to ask someone how much *he* or *she* earns.)
6. Why did you choose this profession?

One last suggestion: Add a professional (and very classy) touch to the interview process by following up with a thank-you note to the person who took time out of a busy schedule to talk with you.

#4 SURF THE NET

With the Internet, the new information super-highway, charging full steam ahead, you literally have a world of information at your fingertips. The Internet has something for everyone, and it's getting easier to access all the time. An increasing number of libraries and schools are

offering access to the Internet on their computers. In addition, companies such as America Online and CompuServe have made it possible for anyone with a home computer to surf the World Wide Web.

A typical career search will land everything from the latest news on developments in the field and course notes from universities to museum exhibits, interactive games, educational activities, and more. You just can't beat the timeliness or the variety of information available on the Net.

One of the easiest ways to track down this information is to use an Internet search engine, such as Yahoo! Simply type in the topic you are looking for, and in a matter of seconds, you'll have a list of options from around the world. It's fun to browse—you never know what you'll come up with.

To narrow down your search a bit, look for specific websites, forums, or chatrooms that are related to your topic in the following publications:

Hahn, Harley. *Harley Hahn's Internet and Web Yellow Pages.* Berkeley, Calif.: Osborne McGraw Hill, 1999.

Turner, Marcia Layton, and Audrey Seybold. *Official World Wide Web Yellow Pages.* Indianapolis: Que, 1999.

Polly, Jean Armour. *The Internet Kids and Family Yellow Pages.* Berkeley, Calif.: Osborne McGraw Hill, 1999.

To go on-line at home you may want to compare two of the more popular on-line services: America Online and CompuServe. Please note that there is a monthly subscription fee for using these services. There can also be extra fees attached to specific forums and services, so *make sure you have your parents' OK before you sign up.* For information about America Online call 800-827-6364. For information about CompuServe call 800-848-8990. Both services frequently offer free start-up deals, so shop around.

There are also many other services, depending on where you live. Check your local phone book or ads in local computer magazines for other service options.

Before you link up, keep in mind that many of these sites are geared toward professionals who are already working in a particular field. Some of the sites can get pretty technical. Just use the experience as a chance to nose around the field, hang out with the people who are tops in the field, and think about whether or not you'd like to be involved in a profession like that.

Specific sites to look for are the following:

Professional associations. Find out about what's happening in the field, conferences, journals, and other helpful tidbits.

Schools that specialize in this area. Many include research tools, introductory courses, and all kinds of interesting information.

Government agencies. Quite a few are going high-tech with lots of helpful resources.

Websites hosted by experts in the field (this seems to be a popular hobby among many professionals). These websites are often as entertaining as they are informative.

If you're not sure where to go, just start clicking around. Sites often link to other sites. You may want to jot down notes about favorite sites. Sometimes you can even print out information that isn't copyright-protected; try the print option and see what happens.

Be prepared: Surfing the Internet can be an addicting habit! There is so much great information. It's a fun way to focus on your future.

#5 SHADOW A PROFESSIONAL

Linking up with someone who is gainfully employed in a profession that you want to explore is a great way to find out what a career is like. Following someone around while the person are at work is called "shadowing." Try it!

This process involves three steps.

1. Find someone to shadow. Some suggestions include
   ☼ the person you interviewed (if you enjoyed talking with him or her and feel comfortable about asking the person to show you around the workplace)
   ☼ friends and neighbors (you may even be shocked to discover that your parents have interesting jobs)
   ☼ workers at the chamber of commerce may know of mentoring programs available in your area (it's a popular concept, so most larger areas should have something going on)
   ☼ someone at your local School-to-Work office, the local Boy Scouts Explorer program director (this is available to girls too!), or your school guidance counselor
2. Make a date. Call and make an appointment. Find out when is the best time for arrival and departure. Make arrangements with a parent or other respected adult to go with you and get there on time.
3. Keep your ears and eyes open. This is one time when it is OK to be nosy. Ask

questions. Notice everything that is happening around you. Ask your host to let you try some of the tasks he or she is doing.

The basic idea of the shadowing experience is to put yourself in the other person's shoes and see how they fit. Imagine yourself having a job like this 10 or 15 years down the road. It's a great way to find out if you are suited for a particular line of work.

BE CAREFUL OUT THERE!

Two cautions must accompany this recommendation. First, remember the stranger danger rules of your childhood. NEVER meet with anyone you don't know without your parents' permission and ALWAYS meet in a supervised situation—at the office or with your parents.

Second, be careful not to overdo it. These people are busy earning a living, so respect their time by limiting your contact and coming prepared with valid questions and background information.

PLAN B

If shadowing opportunities are limited where you live, try one of these approaches for learning the ropes from a professional.

Pen pals. Find a mentor who is willing to share information, send interesting materials, or answer specific questions that come up during your search.

Cyber pals. Go on-line in a forum or chatroom related to the profession you're interested in. You'll be able to chat with professionals from all over the world.

If you want to get some more on-the-job experience, try one of these approaches.

Volunteer to do the dirty work. Volunteer to work for someone who has a job that interests you for a specified period of time. Do anything—filing, errands, emptying trash cans—that puts you in contact with professionals. Notice every tiny detail about the profession. Listen to the lingo they use in the profession. Watch how they perform their jobs on a day-to-day basis.

Be an apprentice. This centuries-old job training method is making a comeback. Find out if you can set up an official on-the-job training program to gain valuable experience. Ask professional associations about apprenticeship opportunities. Once again, a School-to-Work program can be a great asset. In many areas, they've established some very interesting career training opportunities.

Hire yourself for the job. Maybe you are simply too young to do much in the way of on-the-job training right now. That's OK. Start learning all you can now and you'll be ready to really wow them when the time is right. Make sure you do all the Try It Out activities included for the career(s) you are most interested in. Use those activities as a starting point for creating other projects that will give you a feel for what the job is like.

WHAT'S NEXT?

Have you carefully worked your way through all of the suggested activities? You haven't tried to sneak past anything, have you? This isn't a place for shortcuts. If you've done the activities, you're ready to decide where you stand with each career idea. So what is it? Green light? See page 168. Yellow light? See page 167. Red light? See page 166. Find the spot that best describes your response to what you've discovered about this career idea and plan your next move.

RED LIGHT

So you've decided this career is definitely not for you—hang in there! The process of elimination is an important one. You've learned some valuable career planning skills; use them to explore other ideas. In the meantime, use the following road map to chart a plan to get beyond this "spinning your wheels" point in the process.

Take a variety of classes at school to expose yourself to new ideas and expand the options. Make a list of courses you want to try.

Get involved in clubs and other after-school activities (like 4-H or Boy Scout Explorers) to further develop your interests. Write down some that interest you.

Read all you can find about interesting people and their work. Make a list of people you'd like to learn more about.

Keep at it. Time is on your side. Finding the perfect work for you is worth a little effort. Once you've crossed this hurdle, move on to the next pages and continue mapping out a great future.

YELLOW LIGHT

Proceed with caution. While the idea continues to intrigue you, you may wonder if it's the best choice for you. Your concerns are legitimate (listen to that nagging little voice inside!).

Maybe it's the training requirements that intimidate you. Maybe you have concerns about finding a good job once you complete the training. Maybe you wonder if you have what it takes to do the job.

At this point, it's good to remember that there is often more than one way to get somewhere. Check out all the choices and choose the route that's best for you. Use the following road map to move on down the road in your career planning adventure.

Make two lists. On the first, list the things you like most about the career you are currently investigating. On the second, list the things that are most important to you in a future career. Look for similarities on both lists and focus on careers that emphasize these similar key points.

Current Career	Future Career
☼ _____	☼ _____
☼ _____	☼ _____

What are some career ideas that are similar to the one you have in mind? Find out all you can about them. Go back through the exploration process explained on pages 139 to 148 and repeat some of the exercises that were most valuable.

☼ _____
☼ _____
☼ _____
☼ _____

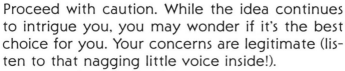

WRITE YOUR RESPONSES ON A SEPARATE PIECE OF PAPER

Visit your school counselor and ask him or her which career assessment tools are available through your school. Use these to find out more about your strengths and interests. List the date, time, and place for any assessment tests you plan to take.

- ☼ _____
- ☼ _____
- ☼ _____
- ☼ _____

WRITE YOUR RESPONSES ON A SEPARATE PIECE OF PAPER

What other adults do you know and respect to whom you can talk about your future? They may have ideas that you've never thought of.

- ☼ _____
- ☼ _____
- ☼ _____
- ☼ _____

WRITE YOUR RESPONSES ON A SEPARATE PIECE OF PAPER

What kinds of part-time jobs, volunteer work, or after-school experiences can you look into that will give you a chance to build your skills and test your abilities? Think about how you can tap into these opportunities.

- ☼ _____
- ☼ _____
- ☼ _____
- ☼ _____

WRITE YOUR RESPONSES ON A SEPARATE PIECE OF PAPER

GREEN LIGHT

Yahoo! You are totally turned on to this career idea and ready to do whatever it takes to make it your life's work. Go for it!

Find out what kinds of classes you need to take now to prepare for this career. List them here.

- ☼ _____
- ☼ _____
- ☼ _____
- ☼ _____

WRITE YOUR RESPONSES ON A SEPARATE PIECE OF PAPER

What are some on-the-job training possibilities for you to pursue? List the company name, a person to contact, and the phone number.

    ☼ _____

    ☼ _____

    ☼ _____

    ☼ _____

Find out if there are any internship or apprenticeship opportunities available in this career field. List contacts and phone numbers.

    ☼ _____

    ☼ _____

    ☼ _____

    ☼ _____

What kind of education will you need after you graduate from high school? Describe the options.

    ☼ _____

    ☼ _____

    ☼ _____

    ☼ _____

No matter what the educational requirements are, the better your grades are during junior and senior high school, the better your chances for the future.

Take a minute to think about some areas that need improvement in your schoolwork. Write your goals for giving it all you've got here.

    ☼ _____

    ☼ _____

    ☼ _____

    ☼ _____

Where can you get the training you'll need? Make a list of colleges, technical schools, or vocational programs. Include addresses so that you can write to request a catalog.

- ☼ _____
- ☼ _____
- ☼ _____
- ☼ _____

WRITE YOUR RESPONSES ON A SEPARATE PIECE OF PAPER

HOORAY! YOU DID IT!

This has been quite a trip. If someone tries to tell you that this process is easy, don't believe it. Figuring out what you want to do with the rest of your life is heavy stuff, and it should be. If you don't put some thought (and some sweat and hard work) into the process, you'll get stuck with whatever comes your way.

You may not have things planned to a T. Actually, it's probably better if you don't. You'll change some of your ideas as you grow and experience new things. And, you may find an interesting detour or two along the way. That's OK.

The most important thing about beginning this process now is that you've started to dream. You've discovered that you have some unique talents and abilities to share. You've become aware of some of the ways you can use them to make a living—and, perhaps, make a difference in the world.

Whatever you do, don't lose sight of the hopes and dreams you've discovered. You've got your entire future ahead of you. Use it wisely.

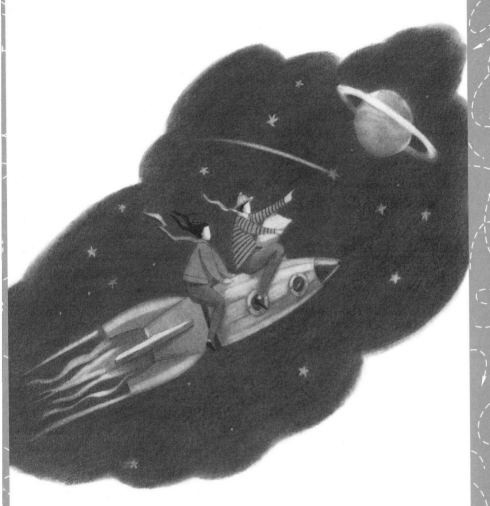

SOME FUTURE DESTINATIONS

Wow! You've really made tracks during this whole process. Now that you've gotten this far, you'll want to keep moving forward to a great future. This section will point you toward some useful resources to help you make a conscientious career choice (that's just the opposite of falling into any old job on a fluke).

IT'S NOT JUST FOR NERDS

The school counselor's office is not just a place where teachers send troublemakers. One of its main purposes is to help students like you make the most of your educational opportunities. Most schools will have a number of useful resources, including career assessment tools (ask about the Self-Directed Search Career Explorer or the COPS Interest Inventory—these are especially useful assessments for people your age). There may also be a stash of books, videos, and other helpful materials.

Make sure no one's looking and sneak into your school counseling office to get some expert advice!

AWESOME INTERNET CAREER RESOURCES

Your parents will be green with envy when they see all the career planning resources you have at your fingertips. Get ready to hear them whine, "But they didn't have all this stuff when I was a kid." Make the most of these cyberspace opportunities.

- Future Scan includes in-depth profiles on a wide variety of career choices and expert advice from their "Guidance Gurus." Check it out at http://www.futurescan. com.
- For up-to-the-minute news on what's happening in the world of work, visit *Career Magazine*'s website at http://www.careermag.com.
- Monster.com, one of the web's largest job search resources, hosts a site called Monster Campus at http://campus.monster.com. There are all kinds of career information, college stuff, and links to jobs, jobs, jobs!
- Find links to all kinds of career information at http://careerplanning.about.com. You'll have to use your best detective skills to find what you want, but there is a lot of good information to be found on this site.

☀ Even Uncle Sam wants to help you find a great career. Check out the Department of Labor's Occupational Outlook Handbook for in-depth information on approximately 250 occupations at http://www.bls.gov/ocohome.htm.

☀ Buffalo State University hosts an exceptionally good career exploration website. Find it at http://www.sny-buf.edu/~cdc/explore.html.

☀ Another fun site for the inside scoop on a wide variety of career options is found at http://www.jobprofiles.com.

☀ Pick a favorite career and find out specific kinds of information such as wages and trends at http://www.acinet.org/acinet/.

IT'S NOT JUST FOR BOYS

Boys and girls alike are encouraged to contact their local version of the Boy Scouts Explorer program. It offers exciting on-the-job training experiences in a variety of professional fields. Look in the white pages of your community phone book for the local Boy Scouts of America program.

MORE CAREER BOOKS ESPECIALLY FOR MUSIC MAKERS

There's a symphony of ways to enjoy earning a living using musical talent and dance skills. See what some of these books have to say about a career in music:

———————————

Baskerville, David. *Music Business Handbook & Career Guide.* Thousand Oaks, Calif.: Sage Publishing, 1995.

Camenson, Blythe. *Great Jobs for Art Majors.* Lincolnwood, Ill.: VGM Career Horizons, 1997.

Des Pres, Josquin, and Mark Landsman. *Creative Careers in Music.* New York: Allworth Press, 2000.

Eberts, Marjorie. *Careers for Culture Lovers and Other Artsy Types.* Lincolnwood, Ill.: VGM Career Horizons, 1999.

Field, Shelly. *Career Opportunities in the Music Industry.* New York: Facts On File, 1995, 2000.

Fink, Michael. *Inside the Music Industry: Creativity, Process, and Business.* New York: Macmillan, 1996.

Goldberg, Jan. *Great Jobs for Music Majors.* Lincolnwood, Ill.: NTC Publishing Group, 1997.

———. *Great Jobs for Theater Majors.* Lincolnwood, Ill.: VGM Career Horizons, 1998.

Haubenstock, Susan H., and David Joselit. *Career Opportunities in Art.* New York: Facts On File, 1995.

Johnson, Jeff. *Careers for Music Lovers and Other Tune Types.* Lincolnwood, Ill.: VGM Career Horizons, 1996.

Krasilovsky, M. William, Sidney Shemel, and John Gross. *The Business of Music: The Definitive Guide to the Music Industry.* New York: Watson-Guptill Publishing, 2000.

Pressman, Donald S. *All You Need to Know About the Music Business.* New York: Simon & Schuster, 1999.

HEAVY-DUTY RESOURCES

Career encyclopedias provide general information about a lot of professions and can be a great place to start a career search. Those listed here are easy to use and provide useful information about nearly a zillion different jobs. Look for them in the reference section of your local library.

Cosgrove, Holli, ed. *Career Discovery Encyclopedia: 2000 Edition.* Chicago: J. G. Ferguson Publishing Company, 2000.

Hopke, William. *Encyclopedia of Careers and Vocational Guidance.* Chicago: J. G. Ferguson Publishing Company, 1999.

Maze, Marilyn, Donald Mayall, and J. Michael Farr. *The Enhanced Guide for Occupational Exploration: Descriptions for the 2,800 Most Important Jobs.* Indianapolis: JIST Works, 1995.

VGM's Career Encyclopedia. Lincolnwood, Ill.: VGM Career Books, 1997.

FINDING PLACES TO WORK

Use resources like these to find your way around the music industry. They include lists of employers and organizations that offer opportunities for musicians, dancers, and other performing artists.

Clark, Sedgewick, ed. *Musical America: International Directory of the Performing Arts.* Hightstown, N.J.: Primedia Information, Inc. 2000.

Cummings, David M. *International Who's Who in Music and Musicians' Directory.* New York: Taylor & Francis, 1998.

Film Producers, Studio Agents, and Casting Directors Guide. Los Angeles: Lone Eagle Publishing, 2000.

Horton, Tara. *Song Writer's Market: 1,600 Places to Market Your Songs.* Cincinnati. Writers Digest Books, 2000.

LeCompte, Michelle. *Job Hunter's Sourcebook: Where to Find Employment Leads and Other Job Search Resources.* Detroit: Gale Research, 1996.

Also consult the Job Bank series (Holbrook, Mass.: Adams Media Group). Adams publishes separate guides for Atlanta, Seattle, and many major points in between. Ask your local librarian if the library has a guide for the biggest city near you.

FINDING PLACES TO PRACTICE JOB SKILLS

An apprenticeship is an official opportunity to learn a specific profession by working side by side with a skilled professional. As a training method, it's as old as the hills, and it's making a comeback in a big way because people are realizing that doing a job is simply the best way to learn a job.

An internship is an official opportunity to gain work experience (paid or unpaid) in an industry of interest. Interns are more likely to be given entry-level tasks but often have the chance to rub elbows with people in key positions within a company. In comparison to an apprenticeship, which offers very detailed training for a specific job, an internship offers a broader look at a particular kind of work environment.

Both are great ways to learn the ropes and stay one step ahead of the competition. Consider it dress rehearsal for the real thing!

Anselm, John. *The Yale Daily News Guide to Internships.* New York: Kaplan, 1999.

Landes, Michael. *The Back Door Guide to Short Term Job Adventures: Internships, Extraordinary Experiences, Seasonal Jobs, Volunteering, Work Abroad.* Berkeley, Calif.: Ten Speed Press, 1997.

Oakes, Elizabeth H. *Ferguson's Guide to Apprenticeship Programs.* Chicago: J. G. Ferguson Publishing Company, 1998.

Oldman, Mark. *America's Top Internships.* New York: Princeton Review, 1999.

———. *The Internship Bible.* New York: Princeton Review, 1998.

Peterson's Internships 2000. Princeton, N.J.: Peterson's Guides, 1999.

Peterson's Internships 1999: More Than 50,000 Opportunities to Get an Edge in Today's Competitive Job Market. Princeton, N.J.: Peterson's Guides, 1998.

NO-COLLEGE OCCUPATIONS

Some of you will be relieved to learn that a college degree is not the only route to a satisfying, well-paying career. Whew! If you'd rather skip some of the schooling and get down to work, here are some books you need to consult.

Abrams, Kathleen S. *Guide to Careers Without College.* Danbury, Conn.: Franklin Watts, 1995.

Corwen, Leonard. *College Not Required: 100 Great Careers That Don't Require a College Degree.* New York: Macmillan, 1995.

Farr, J. Michael, *America's Top Jobs for People Without College Degrees.* Indianapolis: JIST Works, 1998.

Unger, Harlow G. *But What If I Don't Want to Go to College?: A Guide to Successful Careers through Alternative Education.* New York: Facts On File, 1998.

INDEX

Page numbers in **boldface** indicate main articles. Page numbers in *italics* indicate photographs.